SPEEDWAY IN
MANCHESTER

1927-1945

SPEEDWAY IN MANCHESTER

1927-1945

Trevor James & Barry Stephenson

TEMPUS

First published 2003

PUBLISHED IN THE UNITED KINGDOM BY:
Tempus Publishing Ltd
The Mill, Brimscombe Port
Stroud, Gloucestershire GL5 2QG

PUBLISHED IN THE UNITED STATES OF AMERICA BY:
Tempus Publishing Inc.
2 Cumberland Street
Charleston, SC 29401

British Library Cataloguing in Publication Data.
A catalogue record for this book is available from the British Library.

ISBN 0 7524 3000 9

Typesetting and origination by Tempus Publishing.
Printed in Great Britain by Midway Colour Print, Wiltshire.

CONTENTS

INTRODUCTION

Perhaps the most surprising comment that we can make about this book is, 'Why has it not been done already?' For ten years, we have toyed with the idea but taken it no further. 'Why it has not been done already?' is a good question. It was a long friendship with the late Frank Maclean, a doyen of speedway's press, which lit the blue touch paper. Often it was suggested that he should put pen to paper. After all, he knew the story far more intimately than we did. Sadly, Frank died in 1994, but we had listened and learned from him. If anything has been omitted, we can only apologise. To write the full detailed account of speedway in Manchester (Belle Vue in particular) would be a lifetime's work.

Speedway in Manchester commenced in June 1927 at Droylsden. After a lull, the sport took off. Audenshaw appeared in 1928 and was quickly followed by White City Manchester, Belle Vue (Kirkmanshulme Lane) and then Salford.

Of all the other tracks, Audenshaw led the most colourful existence. From the opening day, they had a rollercoaster ride. A successful start was short-lived and they soon closed. After reopening in 1929, the problems arose with track difficulties, Sunday racing and, sadly, fatalities. Closed by the courts in 1931, they were never to race again. In the beginning, the other tracks were very successful, but gradually lost their popularity and closed.

The closure of the original Belle Vue track gave the opportunity for the enterprising North Manchester Motor Club to open an operation a short distance away. They gave us speedway's most famous of teams, the Belle Vue Aces. The club continued to press forward, but the shambolic way in which the English Dirt Track League was organised caused them to withdraw from the league scene in 1929. However, they returned refreshed and dominated the 1930/31 seasons in the north of England. A second Belle Vue-based team entered the Southern League in 1931, further progress was made in 1932 and the seeds were sown for an assault on the domestic honours which speedway had to offer.

Belle Vue was to dominate the sport as no other team did. Under the guidance of Eric Oswald Spence, the Aces withstood all challengers over a four-year period. Had they been permitted to enter the London Cup, they would have probably won that too. During this era, the Aces became a feared, but respected, team, earning the accolade of 'The Invincibles' and 'The Finest Speedway Team in the World', both richly deserved.

Their fall from grace was gradual. Deposed as champions in 1937, they managed to keep hold of the National Trophy and ACU Cup. In 1938, the Aces had a barren year with not one piece of silverware, bar the English Cup, which was won by the reserve side.

1939 promised to be a fruitful season for the Aces in all competitions. However, the outbreak of war saw the suspension of racing and the end of speedway for a period of time, or so it was thought. Three weeks later, Belle Vue was back in business and continued to run throughout the war, staging 176 race meetings. Never knowing who was going to turn up was not a problem to Alice Hart, who was now in charge of the speedway. Not one meeting was lost, as Belle Vue served up entertainment which was craved by people in those dark days.

It was not only the speedway that made the news headlines in the pre-war era. Spare a thought for the Belle Vue mascot, a young girl named Audrey, who was refused permission to lap the track prior to racing by the Manchester Education Authority. A gang of eight to twelve year olds had a den underneath the main stand. After reports of thefts, it was discovered that the young lads were stealing items from the Belle Vue Banqueting Halls and hoarding them in the den. They were working for a sort of 'Fagin' type character, who was eventually brought to justice and jailed.

Even in its heyday, when winning appeared so easy, the club suffered some black days. Mercifully, few riders lost their lives, but James Allen, Stan Hart and Maurice Butler all paid dearly with their lives in racing accidents. Clem Cort, Bruce McCallum and Jackie Hargreaves died in separate, non-speedway incidents and tragically never reached their true potential.

FOREWORD

When I was asked to write the foreword for *Speedway in Manchester*, I was at a loss as to what I should say. When dirt-track racing came to Manchester, nobody could have envisaged the impact the sport would have in the area.

From its humble beginnings at Droylsden in 1927, speedway did not take long to hit the big-time. Audenshaw paved the way, with a series of successful meetings in early 1928 at the Snipe Racecourse and had local riders, such as 'Riskit' Riley, 'Slider' Shuttleworth and the Drew brothers, to serve up the entertainment. Their groundwork encouraged White City to take up the challenge and what a success the venture was! Budding stars were queuing to try their luck and it was not long before the first icons of speedway in the north appeared. Arthur Franklyn quickly established himself in the art of 'skidding' and he earned good money for his troubles.

White City soon had a new challenge to face when a speedway track was opened at the Belle Vue Greyhound Stadium. Despite this, White City remained the premier venue, with its rival failing to attract the same level of support. It was at these early meetings at Belle Vue that followers saw the Langton brothers, together with the popular Australians, Vic Huxley and Frank Arthur. Awful weather in August 1928 enforced an early closure and by mid-September the track had closed. To the north of the city, the activity was frantic, as would-be promoters saw the chance to make a killing. Salford was not expected to last too long, but managed to run meetings well into November, with Ron Johnson finding himself as the fans' favourite.

After the disaster of 1928, another promotion decided to relocate the Belle Vue track to a new purpose-built arena, within the Belle Vue Gardens on Hyde Road. On 23 March 1929, the new super speedway opened its doors and quickly became the premier circuit in the city. Salford and White City had, like Belle Vue, entered the newly formed Northern League, but the idea had been flawed from the outset. Tracks closed, or withdrew, on a regular basis, prompting Belle Vue and then White City to pull out after internal wrangling. It became obvious to most people that there could only be one 'big' track; while the others fell by the wayside, Belle Vue flourished.

Slowly, over two seasons, E.O. Spence moulded a championship-winning side that was feared throughout the land. The Aces' riders gained star status in Manchester, with their services eagerly sought after by entrepreneurial figures to open stores and fêtes. On the racetrack, one trophy followed another as they embarked on a run of four consecutive championships and numerous cup successes. Perhaps it was jealousy that prompted calls from rival promotions for the Aces to have riders taken away from them. Second team matches were held in the late 1930s, from which several promising riders emerged. Only the war prevented the Aces from regaining the championship, but even that could not close the Manchester track.

Locals referred to the club as the 'windmill of speedway', in other words it never closed. The loyalty of the riders, who turned up every week, was the main reason for speedway running throughout the war. Many would arrange leave, allowing them the chance to race. Morian Hansen DFC, Eric Chitty and many others deserve full credit for their efforts. Not once was a meeting lost. Beginning and end-of-season meetings had to start early to comply with the daylight times, as no night racing was permitted.

My association with Belle Vue began in 1937, when I watched my first meeting. Even though the Aces had been in decline, they were still a powerful side. I have been an official with the club for sixty years, starting as a pusher during the reign of Miss Hart, to being the clerk of the course, the position I presently hold. When Johnnie Hoskins arrived at the 'Zoo', I even found time for a spot of 'DJ' work. It has been a privilege to be involved with the club during this time. The friendships I have made with riders and the supporters have been lasting ones. What tales the riders could tell you! These men laid the foundations for future generations, enabling them to enjoy the spectacle of speedway racing.

Finally, I would like to thank the authors for allowing me to write this foreword and wish them every success with the book. I am sure that it will rekindle happy memories for all speedway followers, especially those in Manchester.

Alan G. Morrey – Clerk of the Course, Belle Vue Speedway

ACKNOWLEDGEMENTS

This book has been a labour of love for the club we have supported for longer than we care to remember. Invariably, information comes from many different sources, mainly the libraries and newspapers, but also numerous other enthusiasts. The *Ashton-under-Lyne Reporter*, the *Salford Reporter* and the *Manchester Evening News*, *Chronicle* and *Guardian* have all provided essential information. Particular thanks must go to Stalybridge library for their much needed assistance and guidance. However, the archives of Manchester and Salford libraries have proved equally invaluable.

Individually, our biggest vote of thanks must be given to John Pearson. John has provided a constant flow of information; without this, we doubt that the book would have been completed on schedule. Equally, his daughter, Joanne, has put together a superb compilation of 'Belle Vue's best' and also repaired some dog-eared photographs. Many others have made small contributions, for which we are indebted to them.

The influence of the late Frank Maclean has been a driving force, although we would have preferred the maestro to have penned it himself. We hope that our effort would have met with Frank's approval.

Most of the photographs have been drawn from the collections of Trevor James, Barry Stephenson and John Pearson. Mostly, they are prints of C.F. Wallace, whose plates eventually became the property of Wright Wood, Belle Vue's finest photographic wizard. Our special thanks go to Wright's daughters, Margaret Harrop and Kay Randle, who kindly consented to allow the use of the photographs in the book. Thanks are also due to John Jarvis and Robert Bamford for the loan of some material. For some images, it has not been possible to find the photographer's name. However, we do acknowledge your contribution.

We offer our heartfelt thanks to Richard Frost of the *Manchester Evening News*, who has publicised the book in his weekly column.

Finally, Pamela James has been a good teacher and, without her cajoling, the task would have proved a difficult one. Her interest in speedway racing is nil, so how she managed to wade through pages of text, without boredom setting in, is beyond us! She cannot be thanked enough.

1

BELLE VUE
KIRKMANSHULME LANE
1928

Speedway was a booming sport in the north of England, with new tracks appearing on a regular basis. However, it still had not taken a stranglehold in Manchester. Droylsden and Audenshaw had both been short-lived ventures and the White City track at Old Trafford had only met with reasonable success.

International Speedways Ltd, who controlled several London venues, were looking to spread their wings. Birmingham was chosen for a Midlands track and Manchester appeared to be the ideal place for a northern-based track. Negotiations were held and an agreement was soon thrashed out between the two parties.

The Belle Vue Greyhound Stadium on Kirkmanshulme Lane, Gorton, was the chosen venue. Work began immediately, with the track being pegged out and dug away. The base of the dirt track was formed of clinker compressed into a hard surface to assist the drainage. Shale was used for the top surface to a depth of five inches, which was then rolled hard. The grand opening was set for 28 July at 3pm.

Practice started at once, with several local lads wanting to join the dirt track game to seek fame and fortune. One man who made an impression at these early practices was Alec Jackson, later of Wembley fame as the manager of the famous Lions' team. Jackson's four lap times were around the 92-second mark, which was very good when compared to times at White City of 108 seconds. However, Belle Vue was slightly under the quarter-mile per lap length of White City.

The machinery used was varied and it was interesting to find out that DOT, which was a Manchester-based motorcycle firm, had built a special dirt-track machine, which was ridden at practice by a young local rider. Amazingly, his opponent was none other than White City star, Arthur Franklyn, who struggled to a narrow win. This gave high hopes that, with further tests, the DOT machine could become competitive.

There had been a lot of thought put into how many meetings there should be each week. Initially, it was decided that one event per week would suffice. The lights around the circuit gave everyone a clear view. Therefore, it was settled that once the nights drew in, they would hold a Tuesday night floodlit meeting and this would commence in August.

One practice had to be stopped when around a 100 people, who had earlier been refused admission, rushed the gates and congregated around the track to see the spectacle. Racing was suspended until the intruders were removed by police officers.

SPEEDWAY NEWS

PROGRAMME
at
MANCHESTER
SPEEDWAY
28th July, 1928

Prize Money £160

The Management reserve the right to alter or vary this programme without notice.

OFFICIALS
Manchester

Chief Clerk of Course:
Frank A. Hunting, Esq.

Clerk of Course:
R. S. Maybrook, Esq.

Assistant Clerk of Course:
E. O. Spence.

Medical Officer:

A.C.U. Steward:
W. G. Gabriel, Esq.

Judge—A. S. Morgan.
Timekeeper—H. S. Wheeldon.
Assist. Timekeeper—J. Dearnley.
Starter—E. Campbell.
Lap Scorer—A. Walker.
Telephone Steward—W. Thompson.
Pit Steward—F. Hunt.
Colour Steward—E. N. Bloor.

EVENT 1   To start 2.45 p.m.

GRAND PARADE
AND OPENING OF TRACK.

EVENT 2   To start 3.0 p.m.

MANCHESTER HANDICAP
HEAT 1

Rider	Colour	Hdcp.
Charlie Spinks (A)	Red	2 s.
Jim Kempster (E)	White	2 s.
Mart Seiffert (E)	Blue	2 s.
A. Hill (E)	Yellow	5 s.
L. Hickson (E)	Pink	8 s.
T. Ashburn (E)	Green	9 s.

1st.................... 2nd....................

Time....................

1st and 2nd transferred to Event 6.

EVENT 3   To start 3.8 p.m.

MANCHESTER HANDICAP
HEAT 2

Rider	Colour	Hdcp.
Frank Arthur (A)	Red	Scr.
Eric Spencer (E)	White	2 s.
Bert Perrigo (E)	Blue	3 s.
A. Ward (E)	Yellow	7 s.
R. Sadebottom (E)	Pink	8 s.
E. Kingdom (E)	Green	9 s.

1st.................... 2nd....................

Time....................

1st and 2nd transferred to Event 6.

EVENT 4   To start 3.16 p.m.

MANCHESTER HANDICAP.
HEAT 3

Rider	Colour	Handicap
Frank Pearce (A)	Red	2 s.
Jack Parker (E)	White	2 s.
O. Langton (E)	Blue	5 s.
F. Dobson (E)	Yellow	7 s.
S. Allen (E)	Pink	8 s.
J. Boulton (E)	Green	9 s.

1st.................... 2nd....................

Time....................

1st and 2nd transferred to Event 7.

EVENT 5   To start 3.24 p.m.

MANCHESTER HANDICAP.
HEAT 4

Rider	Colour	Handicap
Vic Huxley (A)	Red	Scr.
Noel Johnson (A)	White	2 s.
E. Langton (E)	Blue	5 s.
A. Jackson (E)	Yellow	5 s.
E. Flinn (E)	Pink	7 s.
C. Manson (E)	Green	9 s.

1st.................... 2nd....................

Time....................

1st and 2nd transferred to Event 7.

EVENT 6   To start 3.42 p.m.

HANDICAP
1ST SEMI-FINAL.

No.	Rider	Colour	Hdcp.
1		Red	
2		White	
3		Blue	
4		Yellow	

1st.................... 2nd....................

Time....................

1st and 2nd transferred to Event 17.

EVENT 7   To start 3.50 p.m.

HANDICAP
2ND SEMI-FINAL

No.	Rider	Colour	Hdcp.
1		Red	
2		White	
3		Blue	
4		Yellow	

1st.................... 2nd....................

Time....................

1st and 2nd transferred to Event 17

EVENT 8   To start 3.58 p.m.

GOLD HELMET
HEAT 1

Rider	Colour
Charlie Spinks (A)	Red
Eric Spencer (E)	White
Bert Perrigo (E)	Blue
A. Ward (E)	Yellow

1st.................... Time....................

1st transferred to Event 15.

Programme cover from the opening meeting in 1928 at Kirkmanshulme Lane.

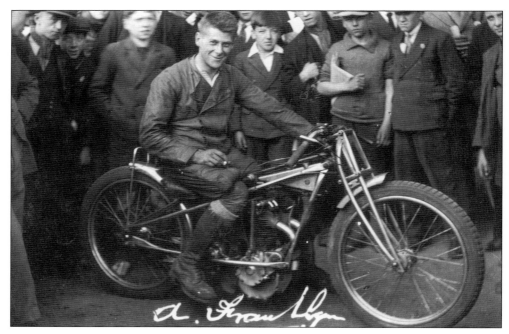

Arthur Franklyn.

Owing to the success of the British Dirt Track Racing Association (BDTRA) track at the White City, International Speedways Ltd realised that the first meeting would have to consist of the best riders available. Vic Huxley, Frank Arthur, Charlie Spinks, Frank Pearce and Noel Johnson would all take part in the opening event. It was hoped that the quality riders on show would draw a good crowd. Eric and Oliver Langton, who were destined to become part of speedway folklore at Belle Vue, accepted the invitation to ride. For Eric, this would only be his third dirt-track meeting, having previously practised at the track. Jack Parker, who became a Belle Vue rider in the post-war era, also appeared.

The main event of the meeting would be the International Speedways Golden Helmet, which was currently held by 'Wizard' Frank Arthur. Admission would be 1s 2d (6p), 2s 4d (12p) and 5s (25p) for the main enclosure.

International Speedways were also looking for a track for training purposes, as the stadium was only available two nights per week. Amongst the options they considered was an offer to use the now closed Audenshaw Speedway – an offer that was not pursued.

On the day of the meeting, International Speedways officials wore some worried looks. The Australian contingent were due to travel by train to Manchester early enough to attend a pre-meeting luncheon at the Midland Hotel, but Vic Huxley came close to not arriving at all. Vic was making his way across London to Euston Station to meet up with the others when his bike fell from the trailer and was damaged beyond repair. The quick-thinking Australian dashed to pick up a bike he had stored elsewhere in London and arrived with seconds to spare before the train pulled out.

This would also be a test as to whether two tracks in such close proximity could co-exist. White City were to hold their usual afternoon meeting on the same day as the Belle Vue opening and it was White City who won the day with a 20,000 crowd as opposed to 12,000 at Belle Vue. That is not to say the crowd were not entertained. After the grand opening ceremony, conducted by Mr William E. Robbins, a director of the International Speedways, the riders were introduced to the crowd, who by now were anticipating seeing this new phenomenon.

International Speedways varied the method in which races were started. Some had a standing start and others a flying start, which confused some of the crowd. Many who attended were doing so for the first time, but they recognised the skill and art of the riders. Warm applause and cheers greeted the riders before and after races, which was greatly appreciated. Track conditions held up well and caused few problems, which allowed all the riders to captivate spectators with their daring and precision racing. Frank Arthur had few problems in retaining his Golden Helmet in a time of 82 seconds from a flying start, compared to a time of 99.3 seconds recorded for a standing start by Jack Parker.

Although they were more than pleased with the entertainment given by the riders, International Speedways acknowledged that they would have to maintain high standards if the Belle Vue track was to be a success. At the same time it was stressed that neither they nor the BDTRA, who controlled White City, wanted conflict. Both

Vic Huxley.

would prefer a healthy, rather than bitter, rivalry. To help foster co-operation between the tracks, International Speedways issued a challenge in which the champion of each venue would race on a home and away basis.

The Australian connection continued at the second meeting. Ben Unwin and Dicky Smythe were brought up from London together with Huxley and Spinks, who had ridden the previous Saturday. The weather may have been glorious, but a low crowd could not have impressed International Speedways. Several new faces made appearances and noticeably they were English riders. Tommy 'Hurricane' Hatch, who was to become a prominent northern racer, made a good debut. Stanley 'Acorn' Dobson rode his second Belle Vue meeting and again acquitted himself well in a quality field.

Finding an answer as to why the crowds were so low was a high priority. It was, therefore, decided to try a midweek meeting to see if a change of race night would work. Manchester's monsoon season forced the experiment to be postponed. This was unfortunate for Vic Huxley, who was again due to ride at Belle Vue. He made an early start, travelling by train to Manchester and arriving at the track in the afternoon. Only then did he realise that he had no racing fuel; Vic preferred to use his own supply. Hasty telephone calls were made to the International Speedways' headquarters for fuel to be despatched by train. The railway company refused to transport it, saying it was a fire hazard. International Speedways immediately sent a car with Vic's fuel supply on a 200-mile, five-hour journey north. Arriving in Manchester, the driver was frustrated to find the journey had been a waste of time.

A big worry for International Speedways was the approaching football season and, with this in mind, they announced that after 11 August, Saturday events would cease. To replace this, there would be floodlit meetings on Tuesdays and Thursdays instead. It was hoped that the new arrangements would show an upturn in the attendance. The management readily acknowledged that running meetings in direct opposition against the nearby White City was not a good idea. They were already established well before Belle Vue appeared on the scene. Supporters would follow their favourites and no amount of persuasion could prise them away from White City; perhaps a change of race day would.

Eric and Oliver Langton were fast becoming the 'darlings' of the track. Oliver had an early success when he won the Silver Armlet at the first weekday meeting. Meanwhile, his brother, Eric, put in some solid performances for a rider of limited experience. Frenchman, Monsieur Gaston, who was a trick cyclist, was booked to display his uncanny sense of direction. His claim to fame was that he could negotiate an obstacle course wearing a blindfold. Previously, M. Gaston had only performed on a concrete surface and the loose track surface provided an extra challenge for him.

Belle Vue once again reiterated the challenge made to the White City previously, which the BDTRA showed a reluctance to accept. International Speedways wanted to match Vic Huxley and Frank Arthur, against Clem Beckett and Arthur Franklyn respectively. White City directors suggested that Huxley and Arthur could accept an invite to ride in qualifying heats and, hopefully, meet Beckett and Franklyn in the Grand Final. This did not cut any ice with International Speedways, who rightly pointed to the public

Frank Arthur, winner of the opening event in 1928.

clamour for these match races to take place. If the Belle Vue pair were to enter the White City event, there would be no guarantee of getting to the final, which made the straight match races more appealing.

Further developments saw White City change their stance. They finally admitted that to match Franklyn and Beckett, who had only been riding for a few months, against two of the best riders at that time, would be no contest. Belle Vue responded by offering to make the races between their two best British riders, which met with the approval of White City. Meanwhile, the planned Tuesday and Thursday meetings were not working. Tuesday was quite popular, but the Thursday night event attracted sparse crowds and was, therefore, unprofitable. With this in mind, the 30 August was the last Thursday staged and, from now on, only one meeting per week would take place – a decision that did not please the Belle Vue patrons.

Perhaps a sign that all was not well came when the management staged a race between two draught horses and two donkeys ridden by the riders – these were desperate measures in an attempt to bolster interest. Many registered their disapproval and showed little interest in this debacle – they took their racing seriously and thought they deserved better treatment than this.

Further problems beset the track surface, which by now was showing signs of wear and tear. Deep ruts had appeared and were causing difficulty with bike control. The season was curtailed early due to the condition of the track and the weather, which was not particularly good. Oliver Langton won the final race for the Silver Armlet. Some

Eric Langton.

12,000 witnessed the meeting, which was far below the expectancy of International Speedways.

At this time, Oliver Langton was far more successful on the dirt track than his brother, Eric, had been. From his prize money on his first night of racing, Oliver had recouped the money (£35) he had paid for his first racing machine. The brothers, who were to become synonymous with Belle Vue during the 1930s, worked well as a team. However, it was in fact to be Eric who became a more accomplished performer, with Oliver tending to busy himself with the mechanical aspects of speedway.

The main question many wanted answered was whether speedway would continue at the stadium. It was obvious that International Speedways were not happy with the way things had gone. The London tracks had worked out very well, as had Birmingham. Manchester folk need not have been worried; already plans had been laid for a new Belle Vue Speedway. The sports ground was situated within the Belle Vue gardens complex on Hyde Road and was a third of a mile away from the current venue. The North Manchester Motor Club was the guiding light behind the venture and had earmarked the site a few months previously. Much planning had ensured that work was done correctly and on schedule.

At a meeting between the NMMC and Belle Vue (M/c) Ltd on 17 October, an agreement had been reached to promote dirt-track racing on the Belle Vue Sports Ground. Within this agreement there was also a clause that granted the NMMC a commission on any gate revenue that exceeded £500.

2

BELLE VUE GARDENS
HYDE ROAD

1929

A permanent standing committee meeting on 4 December 1928 was held at the North Manchester Motor Club (NMMC) offices in Manchester. The members present were E.O. Spence (EOS), S. Chester, A.S. Morgan and H.S. Wheeldon. High on the agenda was the employment of riders together with a riding instructor. Having read the agreement, Wheeldon proposed that Arthur Franklyn be offered the post at a fee of £5 per week, which was unanimously ratified by the committee. A further part of the agreement was that Franklyn should also be guaranteed to ride four meetings a week, with £3 appearance money for each meeting. Two would be at Belle Vue and the others on Northern Dirt Track Owners' Association (NDTOA) tracks.

The NMMC had made known their interest in entering the English Dirt Track League (EDTL) as full members. All of these tracks were affiliated to the NDTOA, who were to run a booking bureau so riders could appear at affiliated tracks. Further meetings of the standing committee were convened to decide future strategy for meetings and to designate official positions for race days.

However, this was not the first motorcycle activity to take place at the Sports Ground. On 1 October 1927, the NMMC organised a grass track meeting on what was to be the centre green of the speedway. On the day of the meeting, heavy rain spoilt the event. Tommy Hatch and Wilf McClure took the honours in the Unlimited and 500cc Finals respectively.

On 25 February 1928, the NMMC utilised the sports ground for an international grass track meeting. Many entrants were to go on to fame and fortune in the speedway. Featuring at the meeting were 'Dusty' Haigh, Alec Jackson, 'Ginger' Lees, Tommy Hatch, Mark Sheldon, Eric Langton, 'Acorn' Dobson and Frank Varey. Also entered in the event were two Dutchmen, K.J. Baar and M Achtien. Various machines were used including a 125cc Francis Barnett and a 989cc Harley Davidson. This meeting was divided into two; a daylight section, running from 2p.m. until 5p.m., and a night section that was held under artificial lighting, commencing at 6p.m. Foggy conditions caused problems in the afternoon, spectators were not able to see beyond half of the one third of a mile course. However, as darkness fell, the fog cleared and forty huge acetylene flares and a searchlight illuminated the track clearly. It is interesting to note that this meeting took place ten weeks before Stamford Bridge held the first floodlit speedway meeting in Britain on 5 May 1928.

Left: *Programme cover for the opening meeting in 1929 at Hyde Road.* Right: *Programme cover from the 25 February 1928 grass-track meeting on the Sports Ground.*

In the afternoon, Wilf McClure won the 500cc Sidecar Final on a 498cc Scott, with the Unlimited Solo Final going to F. Sisson on his 497cc Ariel. At the night event, Oliver Langton won the 500cc Solo on the 498cc Scott. Syd Jackson won the 350cc Solo Final on a 348cc A.J.S. Further meetings were held under the auspices of the NMMC at Belle Vue. The event on the 5 May was blighted by the track breaking up and becoming very bumpy. Clouds of dust obscured the vision of riders and spectators alike. Syd Jackson met with the most success by winning four of the five trophies on offer, with Wilf McClure annexing the fifth one. Two further meetings were held but were closed meetings, with only NMMC members permitted entry into the events. These were held on 7 July and 25 August 1928 and were the last known to take place.

In January, Mr Bernard L. Brook was appointed as track manager, receiving £5 per week. His duties were to oversee the general day to day running of the speedway, although his authority was limited. He had to request any equipment through the speedway committee for authorisation. Brook was responsible for storage of all equipment used at race meetings.

NMMC secretary Wilf McClure donated a trophy to be competed for during the coming season; this became known as the Mancunian Cup. This was to be raced for at the opening meeting. EOS was the driving force; any major decisions had to go through him. He left no stone unturned and was thorough down to the minute details. Over the future seasons the club was moulded in his way.

Club offices had been arranged, together with premises for the pit steward. Even the small matter of a track postbox gained EOS's fullest attention. Chester was given charge for the distribution of prize money and it was agreed that this would be paid in cash. Chester would receive the money from the relevant authorities on race days.

Whether or not juniors should be paid was a thorny question. Some members wanted a Silver Cup and medals to be awarded instead of cash. EOS viewed junior racing as the 'lifeblood' of the club, and he stipulated that *every* meeting in 1929 would have races for junior riders.

Even the first aid services were catered for, with EOS arranging practices and also regular meetings with them to explain the layout of the first aid room facilities. He expected perfection and made every attempt to ensure he got it.

A canteen room had already been built within the pit area and the exact positioning of the tractor shed was left to the surveyor. Provision was made to house the track staff, together with essential equipment they required (namely the rakes and shovels). For their troubles, they were requested to attend regular practice and meetings. Uniforms were provided for all officials and staff, with changing rooms available. Officials were to wear white coats and the pushers wore white flannels and sweaters.

The riders' car parking area was accessed from Redgate Lane and immediately in front of the pit area. Transportation of fans to and from Manchester was arranged; Belle Vue was looking for special trams to ferry supporters. It was a very good idea, with one of Manchester's main tram sheds being located just over a mile away on Hyde Road.

EOS looked into the method of handicapping. He was the clerk of the course and liaised with Brook, the track manager. Both agreed that riders should be handicapped to win and not to lose.

Some things in speedway racing have not changed from the early days up to the present time. In order to limit access to the pit area, a seven foot high wire fence was erected around the perimeter. The committee decided that competing riders would receive passes for themselves and their mechanics. Any abuse of this rule would result in the pass being withdrawn from use. Insurance cover for the riders was another important factor; Mr Morgan had arranged for MacGowan, Glidwell and co to be entrusted with this. They also provided cover for track officials. Publicity was now becoming a very important factor; EOS took the responsibility for this.

At a committee meeting held on 14 February, Mr A.S. Morgan informed those present that Belle Vue had not yet obtained their track licence, although it had been applied for. When this did arrive, Belle Vue raced under permit No. 318.

The NDTOA operated a grading system for riders and any appearance money rates reflected the grading. Below is a breakdown of the rates:

Grade A Star Men	£3 per meeting
Grade A Men (within four seconds of the track record)	£2 per meeting
Grade B Men (within eight seconds of the track record)	£1 per meeting

At a later date, Belle Vue decided that any non-graded riders would receive 10s (50p) per meeting. In July, this arrangement was replaced. Any rider would now be paid for the fourth place.

A maximum prize money limit was also set at £80 per meeting, but this was inclusive of league racing payments. John Henry Iles, who was the chairman of Belle Vue (M/c) Ltd, agreed to a request from EOS for a floating bank balance. This was purely for the use by the NMMC for speedway costs only. Any expenditure would have to be covered by official orders and receipts.

Riders' expenses incurred due to travelling from track to track were fixed as follows:

Travel at the rate of Third Class Rail Fare.
Hotel Expenses at 15s (75p).
Meals: 2s 6d (12$\frac{1}{2}$p) each.

EOS stipulated that all track officials must be NMMC members. The committee gave careful consideration before allotting a specific task to any member. Efficiency to perform a duty was considered before the following members were appointed as track officials.

Clerk of the Course	E.O. Spence
Treasurer	S. Chester
Starter	J.W. Campbell
Machine Examiner	M. Gavson
Centre Phone Steward	W. Fearnley
Judge	A.S. Morgan
Timekeeper	H.S. Wheeldon
Announcer	T.E. Mann
Pit Steward	R. Boyes
Lap Scorer	A. Walker

In May, Harry Wheeldon resigned from the Racing Committee. In addition to the above list, twelve pushers were employed who were all members of the club. EOS had the task of instructing them how to carry out their duties. Mr Brook made a request that ten rakers be placed on each bend. Smartness and discipline came high on the priority list with the speedway management.

Arrangements for practice sessions every Tuesday and Friday were announced. To advertise practice nights, Belle Vue distributed five hundred notices around the Manchester area. Babs Nield, who rode on several northern tracks, signed forms to practice at the New Belle Vue speedway. This caused a rethink with the insurance agreements. They now had to get fresh cover to insure any lady competitors; it later transpired that lady riders would only receive cover for practice events. Permission to distribute 2,000 complimentary tickets for the opening meeting met with the approval of the committee. Each member of the racing committee was to receive an allocation.

Some members appeared unhappy that riders who were not members of the NMMC would be riding in meetings. It was decided that nothing could be done about this, except to request riders to join.

The NMMC had given most attention to the track's construction. The shape had been designed for speed and safety. Beneath the cinder surface lay four miles of drainage pipe. The track had been completed in November 1928 and left to settle over the winter months. Over this period, any excess water had been soaked up, leaving the cinder track in peak condition. Views of the racing were excellent from any vantage point in the stadium and this would be important as 20,000 seats were available. Officially, the crowd limit was around 30,000, but in later years this was exceeded many times.

The central character in the pre-war and wartime era of the Belle Vue story was, undoubtedly, Frank Varey – a brave, but no nonsense rider. Anyone who had the misfortune to block his path could expect a rough ride – more likely towards the back of the stadium stands. Varey was forever riding full throttle into the bend, up to the fence before turning the bike. More than once in his career, Frank upset his opponents by the tactics he employed. Yet at the end of the night's racing, the home and visiting riders would sit down to a post-match meal, in one of Belle Vue's banqueting halls.

Invariably, the all-action style of Varey caused trouble for him too. Throughout his career, this colourful character spent many hours in hospitals. Injuries did not seem to bother him too much – he rode on many occasions when others would not have considered it. He considered retirement when his form deserted him, but the lure of

The incomparable Frank Varey.

his beloved Belle Vue was a strong one. Another option offered to Varey was midget car racing, but the idea went no further than that.

During the pre-war seasons, the name of Frank Varey will be constantly appearing. His approach to racing was controversial yet, despite this, he was also a brilliant rider and, most of all, a star attraction. Just like Ivan Mauger in the modern era, the mere mention of his name would put extra 'bums on seats', if only for the chance of seeing him taken down a peg or two. The tough approach also hid the kinder side of Varey. Any rider in trouble with machinery, whether a team-mate or not, would find Frank wheeling out one of his bikes to assist them.

The 23 March heralded the birth of what was to become the most recognised name in speedway circles and one of the finest speedways ever known. The first race on the track was by Arthur Franklyn's mystery riders, who demonstrated their skills to the crowd. After this, a further 27 heats and finals were raced, with the principal winners as follows:

Mancunian Cup	George Hazard
Evening Chronicle Cup	Arthur Franklyn
Golden Helmet	Arthur Franklyn

Belle Vue named the riders who were to represent the club in the English Dirt Track League. They were Wilf McClure, 'Crazy' Hutchins, Tommy Hatch, Alec Jackson, Bob

Juan Pagano.

22

Harrison, 'Acorn' Dobson, Ham Burrill, Frank Charles, Tony Barrett, Arthur Franklyn, Frank Varey, H.F. Hudspeth and H.F. Chiswell. As a team, they rode their initial league match on 4 May against Preston and took a comfortable win by 40-21.

A few of these riders moved on during the season, with Charles and Burrill ending up with the Preston team. Later in the year, when the league system began to fall apart, Charles was one of many banned by the NDTOA for racing at Belle Vue and other unattached tracks, who were considered outside their jurisdiction. Common sense eventually prevailed and the bans were lifted.

At this time, the team had not taken on the 'Aces' nickname – this was still to come. The emblem originated from the winged red ace of clubs of the NMMC. In May, Henry Iles informed EOS that the speedway programme had to be completed by 9.15p.m. and the track manager was to receive a pay increase to £6 per week during the racing season and £4 in the close season. The one stipulation was that the manager must not partake in any form of motor event within a 100-mile radius of Manchester. Riders were given the opportunity to rent a lock-up at the track for £1 for the first month and 10s (50p) thereafter.

Frank Varey had a full race diary every week. It was not an unusual occurrence for him to ride six times a week. Certainly it may have been a punishing schedule, given that motorways were not yet in existence. On the plus side, Frank held a healthy bank balance and was a good advert for the Scott Motorcycle Company at Saltaire.

At this time Belle Vue had a complaints department that was headed by EOS. Any complaints he received would be considered and acted upon if justified. One anonymous rider complained of poor food at top prices in the pit canteen. EOS instructed the track manager to look into this immediately as he did not want anything upsetting the riders' morale.

The thorny problem of membership of the club resurfaced, and it was proposed that EOS should approach any non-member riders and inform them that they would be excluded from future meetings. It was also mentioned that Clem Beckett was racing on tracks outside the NDTOA. It was then explained that Beckett, together with several other riders, were permitted to do so as they held agreements with these 'outside' tracks.

In June, Belle Vue (M/c) Ltd authorised pay increases for certain track officials, who were to receive a 25 per cent increase. An increase in the allocation of complimentary tickets was also granted to several officials.

Issues were now coming to a head on the league scene. From the beginning, the league had suffered from internal wrangling and this led to several tracks becoming disenchanted – to such an extent that the Speedway Racing Committee proposed their withdrawal from the league at a special meeting held at Belle Vue on 6 July. Their reason for arriving at this decision was that league racing was not popular with the Belle Vue public.

Warrington later followed suit and resigned from league racing and, in the coming weeks, was to develop closer ties with the Belle Vue management. This in turn helped their riders to obtain regular meetings. A deputation from the NDTOA met with the committee. Mr Lees and Mr Garth explained their position for wanting a slight increase

Ham Burrill.

in the prize money at race meetings. Although they were accorded a sympathetic hearing, the chairman, Mr Morgan, gave the committee's reasons for not being able to accept this. At this point the NDTOA representatives withdrew. The committee did agree to meet any obligations for away matches, if requested to do so. It was several days before the decision became known to the outside world. Belle Vue rode their last league encounter at Thrum Hall, Halifax on 11 July, winning 37-27. As a result, the NDTOA imposed a rule that would penalise any club by £250 if they withdrew.

In the meantime, Belle Vue was pressing ahead to increase the capacity of the stadium. Work on the construction of two extra stands commenced and they were quite justified in doing so. Nearly every week, people were being locked out, so the obvious solution was to extend capacity. Further extensions were in the offing for the 1930 season with the ultimate aim of having covered facilities for the majority of the crowd.

Rivalry between Varey and Franklyn had now reached fever pitch. The words on everyone's lips were, 'Are you a Vareyite or a Franklynite?' There was no room for any 'middle-of-the-road' fans – you were either in one camp or the other. At times, tensions between the two factions became rather strained. Quite often, there were heated exchanges and a few 'fisticuffs' handed out. This seemed a rather foolish situation to have – there was a need for competitiveness and certainly a need for both riders.

The two had been going head to head throughout the season for the club championship. Each week a race between the pair was the highlight of the night, at the mid-season point they were still on level terms. It was towards the end of the season that Franklyn eased away and edged Varey out.

On 29 August, it was agreed that Belle Vue Speedway should withdraw from membership of the NDTOA. This came about because Belle Vue wanted to run their meetings in a way that suited them and not be accountable to outside influences. However, they did stress that the resignation was tendered in a friendly spirit and they were prepared to work amicably with the Association in the future.

A new set of riding colours was purchased, with one of the previous colours (green) being replaced with a check design. Green, it seemed, was not a lucky colour to have. The club also made a recommendation that all riders have 'leg chain guards' due to an incident that injured a rider. An amendment to the rules was printed in the supporters' programmes and inserted into the NMMC rules. This was, the ACU stated, 'In Match Races, engines may be over 500cc but must not exceed 700cc.'

Belle Vue organised a special championship meeting on 23 September, with the first prize being £110. Naturally, this offer attracted many of the big names and with it a massive crowd. A crowd of 42,000 crammed the stands and terraces, with many more unable to gain entry. Amid scenes of wild jubilation in the crowd, the home favourite, Frank Varey, received his winner's cheque. For Frank, this was very important as he was riding on the speedways for very personal reasons. Firstly, he wanted to buy a house for himself and his family to live in. However, Frank had another more important reason, his mother whom he so dearly loved, had a serious illness and he saw this as a way of earning money to help with her treatment.

In September, chaos in league racing had reached farcical proportions, with others following Belle Vue's and Warrington's resignations. The Liverpool and Leeds tracks quickly followed together with White City. However, Liverpool and Leeds did eventually return to the league.

The White City management decided to throw in their lot with the Belle Vue booking bureau. The aims of the bureau were to provide the members with rides at the tracks that had opted to operate under the auspices of Belle Vue. Amongst those who chose to operate under the Belle Vue banner were Warrington, Gosforth, Nottingham and

Arthur Jervis.

Frank Varey in spectacular action.

White City, Manchester. Rumours that Sheffield was to operate with Belle Vue proved unfounded at the time.

It was not only teams that came over to Belle Vue. Many individuals made approaches to join the bureau. Plans were being formulated for a new league in 1930, but as a league match only consisted of nine heats, a further twenty races were required to make up a full programme. To do this, Belle Vue wanted the best riders to enter into these trophy races and, having the 'booking system', offered them a means of sustaining this. Some of the notable acquisitions included Arthur Jervis from White City and Bruce McCallum, who was later to die in tragic circumstances.

On 3 October, Belle Vue appointed its first official track photographer, Mr C.F. Wallace of 16 Craig Street, Ardwick, Manchester. At the same meeting, a letter was read out from the Inland Revenue about taxation due and a reply was sent stating that nothing could yet be finalised, as the speedway season was still in progress.

It was decided that the season would carry on, weather permitting, until the end of October. This would have been a convenient time to curtail racing due to many of the

Belle Vue stars being en route to South America for a season of racing in the southern hemisphere. On 10 October, Belle Vue hosted a farewell dinner for Varey, Franklyn and Jervis, who were to sail to Argentina.

An announcement that Belle Vue was to take over the White City came as no surprise, considering the two had been working closely for a month or so. The plans were to change the track entirely by making it bigger. Also it was to be relocated on the outside of the dog track.

The rumours of a new league gained momentum, with several meetings being held in Manchester. Belle Vue was requested by the ACU to send a representative for the promoters' meeting in London on 21 November. EOS was elected to attend this meeting and take any relevant action.

News of an injury to star man Varey was received at Belle Vue. Frank had taken a heavy tumble and sustained a broken shoulder and ribs, together with concussion. It was on this trip that Varey was dubbed by the Argentinians 'El Diablo Rojo' (the red devil) because of the red sweater Frank wore.

During the course of the season, Belle Vue had successfully run 66 meetings, a figure that has never been bettered in the club's history.

An Argentine programme cover.

1930

Plans for the 1930 season were well in hand early on. The Northern League was now established, with a Southern section also operating. Changes had occurred on the NMMC Speedway Racing Committee on 13 February with the resignation of the chairman, Mr A.S. Morgan. It was proposed by Wilf McClure that EOS assume the role of NMMC Speedway Committee chairman, which was agreeable to Belle Vue Speedway and other committee members.

Over the winter period, track officials from the previous year were asked to submit any ideas for improvements in the running of the speedway. Some of the suggestions were as follows – A motorcycle ambulance should be made available for the removal of damaged machinery. All riders should draw for starting positions at the pit gate. Improvements in the contact between speaker and public should be made, with perhaps a five minute speedway news update at each interval. Faster method of track grading should be looked into and the track graded more often. White canvas should be fixed to the safety fence and kept white. (The fence was a white stake one with a kick board.) Eventually it was decided to use a wire fence. A maroon should be used to signal the commencement of the meeting.

The previous announcer, Mr Mann, was not offered the position for 1930. Some committee members were unhappy with his delivery of information and sought his removal. His place was taken by Mr J.E. Kemp, who in the past had announced at the Sheffield track.

Belle Vue team line-up, 1930. From left to right, Oliver Langton, Clem Cort, Len Myerscough, Frank Varey, Bob Harrison, Eric Langton, 'Dusty' Haigh.

Len Blunt.

Committee members had given serious thought to certain aspects of safety during the close season. On a few occasions in 1929, accidents had occurred, with bikes still running, whilst lying on the track. Therefore, a directive was issued that all rakers and pushers were to receive full instruction on how to stop an engine. It had, in the past, been an official's responsibility to carry this out and, partly through ignorance, there had been one or two accidents.

Old wounds were reopened when it became apparent that Belle Vue would be recognised by the ACU. The NDTOA, who had not been invited to the promoters' meeting in November, still refused to relinquish their grip on the few tracks they still controlled. A further blow was handed out when the Provincial Dirt Tracks Ltd resigned from the association; rumours of other possible defections made their position look unsure.

When the ACU made it clear to the NDTOA that they were now in control of racing in the north, peace prevailed. Preston, Barnsley and Liverpool were still affiliated to this body and, therefore, would not be permitted to join the league. Realising that they would not be able to operate as a league, the Association was reluctantly wound up. All tracks outside the ACU, therefore, became eligible to compete in the Northern League.

Yet another track came under the auspices of the Manchester club when Owlerton promoter, Edgar Hart, signed a deal that gave Belle Vue a controlling interest in Sheffield. As they now owned White City and Sheffield, a popular thought at the time was that Belle Vue, having signed up a host of star men through the bureau during the winter, would use these resources to good effect by spreading them out between the three teams.

The main riders who represented Belle Vue in 1930 were Frank Varey, Eric Langton,

Oliver Langton, Clem Cort, Walter 'Chun' Moore, Bob Harrison, Arthur Franklyn and Len Myerscough. Jack Chapman made his way from Australia to England to start the 1930 season at Belle Vue.

Speedway engines roared again on 29 March, when Frank Varey, on his return from Argentina, won the Golden Helmet with great ease.

Belle Vue travelled to Marine Gardens, Edinburgh, for the opening league match and came away with a 21-13 victory. For the first time, the team had worn club colours. In keeping with the NMMC emblem, a black body colour sporting a red 'Ace of Clubs' was used. The actual colours of the NMMC were yellow and blue, but the car badge was a red ace of clubs. The most famous body colour in club speedway had been born. The two sibling tracks also rode in new colours. Sheffield had a 'Red Spade' on blue body colour and White City had a 'Black Diamond' on white.

In the meantime, two more star men made their way into the Belle Vue fold, with 'Sprouts' Elder and Eric Spencer signing up. Elder, who was a legend already, did not actually ride for the Belle Vue team and Spencer moved north, after departing from International Speedways. Belle Vue had been employing riders on month to month contracts and was noticeably unhappy with some of the riders' performances. 'Buzz' Hibberd and Frank Duckett were two of the riders discarded by the speedway management.

Starting procedure caused many problems for the club and one of their own stars, Frank Varey, was one of the main culprits. Frank, the wily character, consistently jumped the starts. There appeared to be some reluctance by the ACU steward to penalise him. In one such instance, the steward stopped the race and restarted it from a standing start, instead of a rolling start. Although it was within the rules to exclude a rider after two false starts, the steward was berated for this action by angry Varey fans, demanding his blood. Calls for action gained momentum.

Such was the calibre of riders on the books that junior riders were finding it increasingly difficult to make ends meet. Most race programmes were laden with the 'big boys', who were taking all the available prize money. There were major fears that some would turn to the unlicensed tracks, such as Audenshaw, in order to make money.

In June, Franklyn received a nasty injury when he fell from his machine. Instead of staying where he was, Arthur made a run for the centre green, but was run over by Len Myerscough. This injury put Franklyn out of action until the end of July.

On the league scene, Belle Vue had plundered all before them; that was until arch-rivals White City breezed into Hyde Road. Confident of continuing their unbeaten run, Belle Vue underestimated a determined White City side who took the wind out of the home team's sails. This was the sole defeat of the season, as the White City stunned the home crowd. White City had gained revenge for their recent loss at home against the parent track.

Prior to the commencement of the first race at the Glasgow league match, Glasgow skipper, Andy Nichol, had an unusual accident. The Glasgow pair were practising when Nichol and another rider collided at walking pace. The unfortunate Nichol was taken to hospital with a broken collarbone, but managed to arrive back before the match was finished. During the second half, there was great excitement when Dick Fletcher quickly leapt off his machine as he was being pushed off. Suddenly, the engine burst into flames. Resident firemen extinguished the blazing engine without too much damage.

Recent signing, Eric Spencer, had, by and large, been a huge disappointment. On the other hand, Percy Dunn, Bruce McCallum and Len Blunt had shown excellent form and had good prospects to progress further.

Once again, the plight of junior riders came to the fore. The management announced that they wanted junior riders to ride for no appearance money. How could a junior rider give his services for nothing and rely on the possibility of winning some prize money? After the past problems, some youngsters simply sold up rather than suffer the spiralling costs. Some of the future meetings did not programme junior races at all. EOS justified the measures taken by saying that it was the crowd attendance that showed whether you were right or wrong and, in this case, the decision was correct. There were near capacity crowds every week, proof, if it was needed, that EOS's methods worked.

The impending closure of White City was no surprise and, in an ironic twist, the last event held there was billed as a Junior Test. One worrying factor was the defection of better known riders to race on unofficial tracks. Around fifty had drifted into the shady world of Audenshaw Speedway, which did not have a safety record to be proud of.

On 23 July, Test match speedway arrived at Belle Vue, when England beat Australia by 56-39 in the Second Test. Max Grosskreutz, a future legend with Belle Vue, rode unbeaten. After the success of the Test match, Belle Vue was awarded the Fourth Test on 3 September. This should have been ridden at Sheffield, but the capacity there was

Australian Test star Dicky Case pictured at Belle Vue.

not big enough.

The hierarchy was looking for new challenges for the team. They had all but won the Northern Section at a canter and EOS wanted sterner opposition. He was already wanting to test the water to see what improvements, if any, would be needed to take on the much stronger teams in the Southern Section.

During the course of the season, EOS arranged challenge matches at three London tracks. All were closely fought affairs that ended in defeat. However, the experience of riding at Wimbledon, West Ham and Wembley could do no harm whatsoever. A team called Belle Vue did ride at Coventry and eased to a comfortable win. The riders, who represented the club, were mainly from the now defunct White City and currently owned by Belle Vue. Wimbledon was the first to journey north and, for once, Belle Vue struggled to overcome the visitors, by a slender 27-26 win. Next to try their luck were Coventry, who presented few problems.

As a club, they had the philosophy that bigger meetings created bigger crowds. Anyone who doubted this could compare Rochdale with Belle Vue. Rochdale, who competed in the Northern League, had been suspended. At the time, they were experimenting with on-course betting on races – even with this, they struggled to muster a crowd of 3,000. Whereas Belle Vue's all-star programme attracted 30,000 plus every week.

In September, Australia approached the Test match with renewed hopes that they could reverse the score and how they tried! A determined Vic Huxley showed off his style and class by winning his four heats. Despite his heroics, England stole the victory that some thought should have gone to the Aussies. Again, it was the minor places that counted for the English. Test match speedway really captured the imagination of spectators; train excursions converged on Manchester from all points in the north west. In addition, trips were arranged from London and the Midlands.

Committee members received a letter from Belle Vue (M/c) Limited, suggesting a variation to the agreement the NMMC had with them over the bonus payment made on every gate that exceeded £500. The Speedway Committee, having considered the contents of the letter, sent a reply to Belle Vue secretary, Mr E.A. Duthie. In the letter the NMMC acknowledged that some variation would be advisable in the circumstances. However, they, as a committee, did not have the authority to agree to a revision.

It was also felt that the relationship between all members of the NMMC and Belle Vue (M/c) Limited was not as harmonious as it could be. Therefore, the committee requested that the question be put on hold until an appropriate time to address their members could be arranged. EOS also suggested that a fund should be set aside to cover any possible liability that Belle Vue might incur. The NMMC's auditors, David Smith Garrett and Co., were also informed and advised. The treasurer requested that Belle Vue despatch particulars of the agreement direct to the auditors, which was done.

Belle Vue won the Northern League with ease, with no one team really presenting a stern enough challenge. In 1930, only league matches took place as there was no Northern Cup competition organised. Manchester was living up to the reputation of being the rainy city, with September being a wet month. Some of the Belle Vue boys already had their thoughts on the winter trip to Argentina. The Langtons, Varey and

Great rivals Vic Huxley and Frank Varey.

Junior rider Ray Higson.

Bob Harrison were eager to leave these shores for the warmer climates. Varey had come home early from the previous trip and been threatened with not being invited again. How could they not invite a rider who was a hero with the Argentine public? Late in the season, further challenge matches were arranged with Hall Green, Birmingham and a London side. Both failed to register a win over Belle Vue, who would have their biggest challenge yet when Wembley came later on.

Warrington and Belle Vue had always had a high esteem for each other. Belle Vue fans dubbed Warrington the 'Warriors' whenever the team or riders appeared – Warrington's followers had always appreciated the efforts of Belle Vue when they rode at the Arpley motordrome. A special challenge match was agreed between Frank Varey and Charlie Hornby, from Warrington, that would see the loser paying the prize and expenses money. Varey won the home leg, but Hornby was unable to meet Frank at Warrington due to the inclement weather which also caused the season to end early.

Belle Vue took on the might of Wembley, who had won the Southern League comfortably. Rightly or wrongly, the club built up the clash to be a decider as to who were the overall champions. In reality, this was never the intention and the match was merely a clash of the Northern and Southern champions. For this challenge, the club had to sign extra riders to make up the numbers. In the Southern section, teams were made up of six riders, in the north it was only four. Therefore, Spence signed up Frank Charles, Arthur Jervis and Max Grosskreutz – all previously attached to the White City team. Everyone realised that Wembley were much stronger than any northern team,

Above: *Ivor Creek.* Below: *Jimmy Stevens.*

which made it essential to sign riders to avoid a one-sided match.

In the Wembley leg, the match followed the visit of Nottingham, who, in fairness, were no opposition for Wembley. A good second-half attraction was needed and Belle Vue offered an intriguing challenge. The home side did not have things all their own way, but scraped home 27-20. At Belle Vue, the Wembley side gave a workmanlike performance and not even the Belle Vue big guns could turn the tide. The visitors were worthy winners by 23½-29½, (56½-43½ on aggregate). EOS was gracious in defeat when he could have quite easily blamed Eric Langton and Bob Harrison, who were both absent (South America-bound). Arthur Jervis was due to ride but, for whatever reason, he failed to appear. He found himself in hot water with EOS. Once again he had let the club down by not fulfilling a booking and he was fined for the offence.

For the first time since the track opened, the meeting of 4 October was postponed due to rain. The 57th, and last, meeting of the season took place on 11 October, with Varey ending the season as he had started it, by winning another trophy, the Supporters Cup. Belle Vue had granted the fans the opportunity of having a meeting of their own. After weeks of preparation, they donated the trophy, which was won by Varey.

Towards the end of the season, the up and coming Clem Cort had been experimenting with a DOT Dirt Track engine, but never seemed able to get it motoring properly. The Manchester-based company was eager to get a foothold on the machinery side of the sport.

Riders come into the sport, some stagnate and progress no further, yet others exceed all expectations. In Bob Edwin Harrison, the club had found a rider who made an immediate impact. Bob was born in Mellor, near Stockport, in 1906. As EOS was a well-respected organiser in the Manchester area, he was approached by A.J. Hunting, one

Clem Cort in his Chrysler.

Bob Edwin Harrison.

of the Kings Oak organisers to put forward riders' names for the High Beech meeting in February 1928. He recommended Harrison and Stanley 'Acorn' Dobson. Both men had been successful on the grass-track scene. At the meeting itself, Dobson was the only person Bob knew, so they kept each other company and offered mutual encouragement. Overall, considering this 'Dirt Track' game was a new phenomenon to him, Bob had what could be described as a successful debut on the cinders.

He did not have to hang around in the south for very long because the dirt track at White City Manchester gave Harrison a chance to display his talents. The opening of the Hyde Road speedway saw Bob on the move once again and there he stayed, making slow, if not steady, progress. By mid-season, Harrison began to show the form that EOS had always believed was there. He gave an already unbeatable side, further strength in depth. Valuable experience was gained on his two overseas trips to the Argentine and, in 1931, he was to star initially with the northern team, before transferring to the southern team. The ACU finally caught up with Varey and handed him a £5 fine for jumping the starts. Naturally Frank, being Frank, refused to pay this and promptly left the country, for his South America trip.

Jack Wood, from Bolton, who had been associated with the club for two seasons, ended up in court for riding a speedway bike on a main road. Wood was trying to repair a bike that would not start. In an attempt to get the thing to fire up, Jack pushed it onto the road, when suddenly the engine burst into life. He had no alternative but to run the bike until the fuel in the carburettor ran out. The incident could not have happened in a worse place; he rode by the Castle Street police station speedway-style and was apprehended when he finally stopped. Wood was charged with riding a bike with no brakes, no licence and not having any personal identification. Poor Jack really did not have much evidence in his defence.

Not for the first time, Frank Varey was involved in an accident; sadly this time one

Walter Hull.

that had fatal consequences. Frank was an all-round competitor and also rode at the Isle of Man TT races. Having arrived in Argentina, he entered the Sidecar Agaroil Challenge Road Race and was riding the only way Frank Varey knew how to – fast. Clouds of dust from the leaders made vision for those behind limited, when, suddenly, Varey collided with a horse-drawn water cart. Mayhem followed as the ensuing riders, still unaware of the accident, approached. A second rider, the Argentinian Antonio Gerli, ploughed into the wreckage. Frank was pulled from the carnage and taken to hospital with head, shoulder and hand injuries. Gerli was not so fortunate and he died from his injuries, as did the poor water cart driver.

A Christmas meeting was arranged and held on 26 December. Walter Hull had a good festive season, winning all the trophies. Heavy snow in some parts of Lancashire was causing problems on the roads. Manchester appeared to have escaped the worst of the weather and there was never any threat to the meeting not going ahead. A healthy attendance was treated to some close racing.

1931

In January, the NMMC proposed that a club dinner be held for officials and riders in one of the Belle Vue banqueting halls. This was set for 24 February and Belle Vue chairman, Henry Iles, was formally invited to attend as a goodwill gesture.

The committee came up with an idea to give complimentary tickets to the public. A hot air balloon filled with complimentary tickets was to be released from the centre green. In theory, this presented no problem, with the idea that the tickets would be found wherever the balloon landed. The plan went awry when the balloon was lost and, with it, the tickets.

Track officials were to remain much the same as the previous year. The treasurer submitted a revised list of salaries to be paid in 1931, which was approved by Belle Vue. In most cases, the new rates represented a reduction in pay. The samples of officials' salaries are shown below:

Assistant Clerk of the Course	£2
Judge	£1
Timekeeper	£1
Announcer	£1
Starter	£1
Chief Pusher	£1
Pushers	8s 6d (42½p)

Belle Vue Southern in 1931. From left to right, back row: Len Blunt, Arthur Franklyn, Chun Moore, Eric Gregory, Max Grosskreutz. Front row: Reg West, James 'Indian' Allen.

PROGRAMME COPYRIGHT

North Manchester Motor Club

PRESIDENT: J. HENRY ILES, ESQ.

PROGRAMME

BELLE VUE SPEEDWAY

Saturday, August 1st, 1931,

At 7-0 p.m.

The Management reserve the right to alter or vary this Programme without notice.
Held under the General Competition and Special Track Rules of the Auto Cycle Union, together with the Supplementary Regulations of the Club.

Track Licence No. 318.   Permit No. T.A. 206.

The A.C.U. Official Measurement of the Track is 418 yards.

Racing Manager: E. O. SPENCE

OFFICIALS.

A.C.U. Steward	A. TAYLOR
Clerk-of-the-Course	E. O. SPENCE
Judge	W. H. S. ANDREW
Starter	W. CAMPBELL
Timekeeper (A.C.U. Appointment)	H. S. WHEELDON
Assistant Timekeeper	W. E. McCLURE
Announcer	J. E. KEMP
Pit Steward and Mechanical Sup.	MAURICE GAVSON
Treasurer	S. CHESTER
Deputy Official	R. S. BRAND

SPECIAL HOLIDAY MEETING
AUGUST BANK HOLIDAY
AT SEVEN P.M.

JOIN THE SUPPORTERS' CLUB NOW

Annual Subscription, 1/6.   Get your Badge and Membership Card from the Track Manager to-night

"JOHNNY," our TEAM MASCOT, was kindly presented by Mr. FRED LAMB, of the "Preeless" Bulldog Kennels, Altrincham.

Mr Bernard L. Brook, the track manager, informed the committee in writing that he desired an increase in excess of the agreement he had already. A reply was sent to Brook agreeing the increase could be justified.

The allocation of complimentary tickets to officials was restricted to committee members, who were to receive twelve for each meeting. EOS was perturbed as some officials were not attending practice sessions. He was adamant that this situation must be rectified. Any absenteeism would first result in a reprimand and then, perhaps, dismissal.

Since the track had opened, a proper ambulance room had not been provided. Therefore, it was put forward that this matter be given serious consideration. The track doctor had made representations to EOS, who readily agreed to take the matter to Henry Iles. After a meeting, both parties acknowledged that a first aid room should be constructed.

The following riders were all attached to Belle Vue during 1930, but rode for other tracks in 1931:

Sheffield	'Dusty' Haigh, Norman Hartley
Leicester Super	Cliff Watson, George Hazard, Alby Taylor
Leeds	Frank Charles, Len Myerscough, Bruce McCallum
Glasgow	Percy Dunn
Wimbledon	Clem Cort

In total, Belle Vue had over 55 riders on their books for 1931 – it was little wonder that many struggled to get rides at the track. Other riders who transferred from Belle Vue were:

'Sprouts' Elder – An application by Southampton was received for his transfer. Elder had captained the Southampton team in 1930.

Ernie Evans – He had been associated with Belle Vue in 1930, but was transferred to Wimbledon for the 1931 season.

Percy Dunn and George Hazard – Stamford Bridge found themselves with insufficient riders for the National Trophy Final against Wembley. In order to field the team of 8, plus 2 reserves, these two riders transferred to ease the rider crisis. Percy Dunn had returned to Belle Vue when Glasgow shut down and George Hazard had reverted to Belle Vue when Leicester Super closed down.

During the winter, special consideration had been given to the track surface. There had been quite a few complaints from the top boys that it was sometimes rough and rutted in 1930. When the season had ended, the whole track was re-laid and left to Mother Nature for bedding down. For 1931, the Belle Vue racing colours were scarlet with a large white racing number on the front. Above this was a small red ace of clubs with a black outline.

Frank Charles.

Pay rates for the 1931 season were as follows:

Appearance money: £5
League and Cup racing £1 per point: (£3 for a win)
Test Matches: £2 per point (£6 for a win)

Belle Vue opened their season on 4 April with an All Star event. Prior to the main events, four fully masked riders rode at great speed around the Hyde Road circuit in a demonstration race. Then, to the delight of the 30,000 fans, Frank Varey led the riders onto the track. Accompanying Frank was a young mechanic, 'Curly', dressed in a red page-boy uniform, leading the new Belle Vue mascot, Johnnie, an eighteen-month-old bulldog wearing a red jacket. All the Belle Vue riders were introduced to the crowd. It proved to be Frank Varey's night as he won the Golden Helmet from Walter Hull and 'Chun' Moore, before defeating Frank Charles in the All Star Race.

A mention must be made with regard to the camaraderie that existed between the riders, whether they were rivals or not. The two Franks, Varey and Charles, were now in opposing camps, but this did not mean that one would not help the other. Charles was having engine problems before his Silver Helmet heat against his rival. Varey simply wheeled out a second bike for his opponent to ride. Charles was the winner. Again, before their match race, Varey repeated the gesture, but this time they spun a coin to

Jack Chiswell with mechanic Alf Bellamy.

see who would choose each machine. Charles won and picked the bike he had previously rode and duly defeated Varey. Many saw Varey as being a bit of a rough diamond, which he may have been at times. What nobody could deny was the sportsmanship he showed towards fellow riders.

Eric Langton retired at the beginning of the season for a spell. This was not to be a long absence and, after much speculation, he was back 'home' after missing five matches. His retirement coincided with the arrival of the Australian, Max Grosskreutz – was Max perhaps signed as a replacement for Langton?

The Northern League of 1931 bore little resemblance to the previous season. Only Preston, Leeds, Glasgow, Sheffield and Leicester Super remained with Belle Vue. All teams were to meet twice at home and away. Times were hard in the north, unemployment was high and tracks literally disappeared overnight. The main team members for the season were Frank Varey, Bob Harrison, Walter Hull, Oliver Langton, Len Woods, Eric Langton, Walter 'Chun' Moore and a new find, Wilf Mulliner. They had acquired one good rider to add to the many already there. James 'Indian' Allen was transferred from Middlesbrough, however, it was only to be a short but eventful stay for this likeable lad. His career was to end in tragedy. Circumstances that arose a few months hence were to make the large squad of riders justified.

A club was formed under the name 'Manchester Legion of Fans'. Each week there were to be 500 lucky programme numbers drawn, with the winners choosing a tin lapel

Max Grosskreutz.

badge of their favourite rider and an opportunity to 'join the club'. The first official supporters' club was formed at the end of the season.

Special practice nights had been arranged in respect of some forthcoming league matches, these were held on 22 March and 15 April respectively, to cover the Sheffield and Preston away fixtures. The usual Thursday night practice was still in place. They say practice makes perfect, but in this instance it did not as Belle Vue lost both matches.

Preston was seen as being the team that would cause Belle Vue the most problems. Joe Abbott was the Preston star and was quite capable of beating the best at Belle Vue. During the match at Preston, Varey had his expected brush with officialdom. The ACU steward caused a furore by disqualifying Frank, but not giving his decision until after the following race. Apparently, Varey cut in on 'Ginger' Lees, who, he alleged, had done the same to him on the previous lap.

Belle Vue had opened their league campaign against the much-fancied Preston side and the Farringdon Park men certainly gave Belle Vue a scare. In the end, it was one of the lesser lights who won the day. Len Woods went through the card unbeaten, overcoming 'Ginger' Lees and Joe Abbott in two thrilling encounters.

Incidentally, the mouthpiece of Belle Vue, *The Bulletin*, reported that Preston had arrived with their own canine mascot, an aristocratic looking chow, complete with blue and white uniformed handler. Johnnie, it seemed, was not too impressed! The Preston supporters also brought along a toy sheep mounted on a shepherd's crook. This is actually part of

Preston's coat of arms, with the letters 'PP' (Proud Preston) on either side of the sheep.

The defeat at Sheffield caused a change in personnel, when Jack Harris, who had previously tuned Varey's bikes, was appointed as team manager. This was not to be his sole duty as Harris was also given the role of Belle Vue mechanic, responsible for tuning all riders' bikes.

EOS experimented with a novelty item when the team was away at Leeds. His main attraction was a North *v.* South match, made up of match races. All the winners then progressed to a grand final, which was won by 'Dusty' Haigh. He then entertained the crowd with chariot racing which, to be fair, was not met with any hostility. Considering that the main riders were away, a 25,000-strong crowd was excellent.

Club officials received complaints from people who had travelled to Leeds for the league encounter. Most seemed unhappy with the way that the visiting riders had been treated. A hostile crowd did not help matters, with abuse being given out to riders and fans.

The visit of Glasgow for the league encounter caused many problems. They suffered mechanical failures all night. EOS was only too aware of the 9.15 p.m. restriction imposed by Belle Vue. He managed to rush through sixteen after-interval races in 55 minutes, to meet the deadline.

Another promising youngster burst on the scene, in the shape of Wilf Mulliner. EOS encouraged rivalry between the junior riders. One particular evening, Mulliner was battling with fellow junior, Len Blunt. He led most of the race until Blunt committed himself to a do-or-die manoeuvre. Diving underneath Mulliner at high speed, Blunt wobbled as he touched his rival and crashed to the track, with Mulliner keeping control and crossing the line.

Unbeknown to most people there, Wilf had actually been injured in the clash, but he made no fuss about it. When he bravely came to the start in his next outing, the ACU steward halted the start when he noticed that the rider seemed unable to control his machine. In his view, Wilf was not fit to ride and the track doctor was called for. After the examination, the youngster was permitted to take his start. Not deterred by this, Mulliner very nearly earned a placing behind 'Dusty' Haigh, only for Franklyn to nip in over the line.

For the first time, Belle Vue entered the National Trophy event and entertained Wombwell in the first round. From the start, the tie was a non-event, with Wombwell being overwhelmed by 137-49 on aggregate. Southern League Wimbledon was the next opponent.

The Star Championship Qualifying Rounds for the unofficial 'World's Championship', currently held by Vic Huxley, began with eliminating rounds being held at all tracks to decide which rider would go forward. The competition was a forerunner to the individual competition of later years, with the winner recognised as the best rider. Belle Vue arranged a series of match races to eliminate riders, with the eventual winner meeting Frank Varey for the honour of representing the club. The draw was:

27 May	E. Langton beat M. Grosskreutz 2-0
30 May	A. Franklyn beat B. Harrison 2-0
6 June	C. Moore beat W. Hull 2-0
10 June	L. Woods beat R. West 2-0

Wilf Mulliner.

In the next part of the elimination match races, the draw stood:

17 June   A. Franklyn beat L. Woods 2-0
17 June   E. Langton beat C. Moore 2-0
1 July   E. Langton beat A. Franklyn 2-0
15 July   E. Langton beat F. Varey 2-0

In beating Varey, Eric Langton earned the right, as Belle Vue Champion, to progress to the Northern Eliminators. The Northern Eliminators were raced over two legs, the highest aggregate rider being the winner. Eric's first opponent, Arthur Jervis of Leicester Super, was defeated in July. 'Dusty' Haigh of Sheffield was his next victim in mid-September. Langton finally earned the right to challenge Jack Parker in the National Eliminator by beating 'Ginger' Lees of Preston. In the final, Langton lost in both legs by 2-0. Therefore, it was Jack Parker who went forward to challenge Huxley, with Parker winning.

Several riders made the trip up to Barrow-in-Furness for the grand opening of the new speedway at Holker Street. The highlight of the night was the tussle between Varey and Frank Charles, who, for once, was riding on home soil. Charles was born in Barrow on 10 March 1906.

Developments in the Southern League hastened the closure of the Harringay track in early June. They had transferred the crowd favourite, Vic Huxley, to Wimbledon, prior to the closure. The day was saved, or so they thought, when Hall Green, Birmingham agreed to take on the Harringay fixtures. Three days later, Hall Green announced it was closing and this again created major problems for the Southern Section.

Negotiations between Belle Vue and the National Speedway Association (Southern) resulted in the club agreeing to take over the remaining Harringay fixtures. The new team was to be known as Manchester and ride the Southern League matches on a Wednesday evening. A midweek night was chosen to avoid disruption with the already successful Northern Section team. The colours were to be yellow, probably because the colours of the NMMC were yellow and blue. One or two riders would have to 'transfer' to the other team, to give it some stability. The management went to great lengths in ensuring those remaining with the Northern team would still carry enough power to retain the championship.

Altogether, the club would be utilising fourteen riders per week, in order to keep both teams running. This was probably the most important development for the club since it opened in 1929 and also for speedway in Manchester. It was clear that the Southern counterparts wanted a team from the north, not only to keep the league number levels, but as a new attraction.

The league record that Manchester took over was:

P. 14   W. 6   D. 0   L. 8   12 points
6th position in the league

Belle Vue, as a club, was now involved in four competitions:

> The Northern League
> The Southern League
> The *Sunday Chronicle* Northern Knockout Cup
> The *Daily Mail* National Trophy

It was fortunate that they did have a reasonably strong squad from which to select the two league teams. However, when it came to the cup matches, members of both league sides were interchanged. Manchester had the following main body of riders from which to select a team: Arthur Franklyn, Max Grosskreutz, James 'Indian' Allen, Len Blunt, Walter 'Chun' Moore and Reg West.

Sheffield arrived for the return leg of the Knockout Cup with a slender 5-point lead, which was quickly overturned. The aggregate win of 57-49 was rewarded with a semi-final tie against the team Belle Vue feared most of all, Preston. It was proposed to play the tie in July in order to allow both teams enough time to prepare for the final.

Preston had been annoyed when Joe Abbott and 'Ginger' Lees were overlooked for selection into the England Test team. Belle Vue had three representatives and this seemed to be a sore point with Preston's management. A challenge between Abbott, Lees and Wotton was issued by Preston and accepted by Belle Vue. EOS was quick to point out that although he did not pick the Test match riders, he was perfectly happy to go along with the challenge. The interest generated would pull in a large crowd. Preston arrived with a point to prove and won by 14-11, much to the delight of the masses from Farringdon Park. They won the advantage for the Preston leg by 5 races to 4.

In the Northern League, Belle Vue were chugging along nicely, but, unlike the past, were not having things all their own way. Not only was Preston providing stern opposition, a rejuvenated Leicester Super team now came into the equation after a deserved victory at Melton Road over Belle Vue. Frank Charles and Clem Cort returned from Leeds and Wimbledon respectively and rode with the Southern League side. They did make appearances with the Northern Knockout Cup side when required.

The new Manchester team made a poor start and lost in their home Southern League debut against a talented Wimbledon side by 34-20. On the same night, the supporters were given a double helping of league racing. The northern side took on fierce rivals, Preston, and put them firmly in their place. As if to prove the point, they travelled to Preston and came away with two hard-earned points from a hotly disputed match. Cries of foul were heard from the home support when some dubious decisions were allowed to stand by the ACU steward. The wins eased Belle Vue into a comfortable lead ahead of Leicester and Preston.

A junior rider, Frank Burgess (a relation and future mechanic of 1933 sensation, Bill Kitchen), certainly felt the heat in one particular race. Burgess had just won his semi-final, when he suddenly realised his machine was on fire. Burgess got off the bike much faster than he had got on it! The flames were extinguished and, in the final, Burgess cruised to an easy win.

Varey found controversy when 'Chun' Moore was excluded from a race for false starting. Frank came up to the line, but declined to start as the flag was dropped. The remaining two riders pulled up, realising what had happened. In the end, Moore was reinstated, which was to the satisfaction of the crowd and Frank. Inconsistency when making decisions was a major talking point, with starts being the biggest headache. This would not be the last occasion when a steward was swayed by a hostile reception.

Bill 'Tiny' Campbell, the starter, had a horrendous time trying to allow racing to start – the issue was fast becoming a nightmare for officials, riders and the fans. Sheffield's track manager, Ben Sneath, had been present and witnessed the problems that Campbell was enduring. He was moved to compliment Campbell's patience with the situation, but, in line with others, Sneath also wanted to see false starts stamped out.

Manchester broke their duck when defeating Nottingham in the Southern League clash. It was another new signing, Eric 'Smiling' Gregory from Wombwell, who pleased the small crowd of 14,000 with his dashing style. Belle Vue bowed out of the National Trophy on aggregate to Wimbledon, who possessed an all-round strength that could not be matched. However, it was a learning curve that was being observed closely by EOS for future reference.

In a light-hearted moment, *The Bulletin* observed that 'Acorn' Dobson, although now retired, was still hanging around the Belle Vue pit area. It was, in fact, Bob Harrison disguising himself in Dobson's old purple leathers (which had a gold acorn on the shoulder). Supporters were also kept involved with a variety of activities, one such event being a club treasure hunt that was held within the Belle Vue gardens. The prizes would be distributed at various points and could only be found by solving the clues. Items would be hidden at a height of between one and six feet.

A great deal of debate went on amongst supporters over radio broadcasting. The club received much correspondence on this matter. The main query was why big events such as Test Matches could not be broadcast live? Football and cricket were – why not speedway? Live broadcasts were to change this situation in the coming years.

Eric Langton was showing his best form at this time and was a match for any chal-lenger on the sweeping Belle Vue bowl. A great deal of credit should be given to older brother, Oliver, who maintained Eric's motors. Oliver himself was no mean

Frank Burgess.

Dot Cowley.

performer – at the end of June his race points secured in all competitions actually exceeded his brother's.

News that the White City Speedway in Glasgow had closed was a blow to the Northern League as this left only five competing teams. It was decided to soldier on with the remaining league teams, plus the Knockout Cup matches. Some of the White City lads eventually raced with some distinction at Belle Vue. Those who figured prominently were Norrie Isbister and Andy Nichol (who was a full-time coal miner and therefore only rode speedway at weekends).

The Northern and Southern teams met in what was billed as the 'Great Inter-Track Team Duel.' Which was better – north or south? Varey, who captained the northern team, led them to what seemed an unassailable lead until, suddenly, the southern team, led by Franklyn, made a gallant effort to reduce the arrears, but fell three points adrift.

A few days later, the false start epidemic reared its ugly head once again. Naturally, Varey was involved and, for once, the steward was not for changing his decision. Angered by this, the usual pro-Varey crowd demonstration took place, resulting in the poor official requiring a police escort when vacating the premises. The meeting did produce something positive to enthuse about, with Manchester gaining a good win over Lea Bridge.

The away form of Manchester showed the gulf that had to be overcome if they were to match the much better organised teams of the Southern League. It was well known that in 1932, the preference would be to have a single National League operating. Obviously, this would include a Belle Vue/Manchester side, which was possibly the only team of the current Northern Section that could put up a challenge. From the results away from home, EOS was well aware of the changes he would need to make if Belle Vue was to be a force.

Once more, Knockout Cup fever came to Manchester, in the shape of Preston for the cup semi-final. A close match was to be expected. Belle Vue fielded the best of the north and south sides – this alone showed the respect they had for Preston. It was a good job that they did as, for once, Langton had an off night. Going into the last heat with Belle Vue a point adrift, Langton was leading from the start, with Preston holding the minor places until Les Wotton cruelly had a motor failure. This allowed Wally Hull to take the third place and, with it, a 1-point win to the home side. Franklyn should have raced for the side, but he was competing in the King's Cup Air Race.

The return match was no less exciting, if not a little dangerous at times. For several weeks, the condition of the Farringdon Park track had raised a few eyebrows. On the night it was no different, as riders came to grief at the same spot, time and time again. If anything prevented Preston from delivering the ultimate knock-out blow to the visitors, it was their own track. A single point win, this time to Preston, saw the teams tied at 53-53, meaning the whole tie had to be replayed. Both promotions were happy for a replay, especially Belle Vue, who were in no mood to offer a second chance.

Preston did lodge an official complaint over the inclusion of Frank Charles. They claimed that he had already represented Leeds in a previous round, which was a fact. However, two precedents had been set already: York, who were in the Northern Knockout Cup, had 'Broncho' Dixon and Jack Barber riding for them in the competition.

Both had been transferred from Sheffield, for the purpose of riding in the cup, after riding against Belle Vue in the first round. On 9 July, 'Smiling' Gregory rode for Wombwell in the Northern Cup against York, eight days after his Manchester (Southern) debut.

After Preston's complaint regarding Frank Charles, the management agreed to comply with their wishes and withdrew Charles from the tie. The tie did have a nice touch to it. The Preston captain, Joe Abbott, had been injured – in order to assist them, Belle Vue transferred Norrie Isbister for league and cup purposes. How Preston must have rued that missed chance of glory. In the replay, Belle Vue went to town on them and, to be brutally frank, they were annihilated. This was a double-header match featuring High Beech for the first and only time in Manchester. The southern side demolished the visitors with ease to claim the league points. Slowly but surely, Manchester was making steady, if not erratic, progress.

In the cup match, one rider made an appearance and he was to have a profound effect on Belle Vue Speedway within a couple of seasons. A certain William Kitchen had been programmed in the second-half junior races; he won his heat with ease and then the final. Alas, at this juncture, speedway was not high on Bill's priorities. He had ridden in 1929 and wanted to take up speedway, but family ties prevented him from doing so.

On 15 August, an unusual race took place, which was termed in the programme as a pursuit race. Langton, Grosskreutz, Harrison and Woods were to start from points opposite each other, namely the starting line, back straight and in the middle of the bends. The winner would be the rider completing his four laps and arriving at the starting point first. A judge was placed at each point with a gun and a coloured rocket, which would be fired as each rider completed his four laps. It may have been exciting for the fans, but it was confusing for the officials. Langton won the race, but the experiment never went any further.

The all-star Wembley team travelled north for a match they ought to have won. On the day, it rained as it can only rain in Manchester. The weather frustrated the Wembley side, who won eight of the nine races. Frank Charles was the only Manchester race winner – he and 'Indian' Allen won the match, with a maximum heat advantage. In fairness, Wembley were out of luck all night as mud and water cut out engines with regularity.

Matters came to a head when one of the visitors kicked over a bucket of water in temper. A punch was thrown at an official when he reprimanded the rider. The official was dazed and received aid from his colleagues. Belle Vue was annoyed that the rider was allowed to continue the match, after the ACU steward was alerted about the incident. Manchester had surprised many by winning the match by 28-26, even though conditions were atrocious.

On 22 August, the Belle Vue and Manchester teams were involved in four meetings on one day. Manchester rode an afternoon meeting at High Beech before travelling to Stamford Bridge in the evening. Both league matches ended with comprehensive defeats. Meanwhile the northern team played hosts to Sheffield in a challenge and it was the visitors who scored a surprise win. Preston invited Belle Vue to send a reserve side for a challenge. This was a mistake by the Preston management – the low crowd who attended saw Preston defeated 30-24.

Airman – Arthur Franklyn.

A week later, Preston had Belle Vue as visitors again. This time Belle Vue was determined to qualify for the final against Leeds. The largest crowd for weeks saw the plucky home team go down fighting. An aggregate win by 66-42 put Belle Vue in the final. During the meeting, Walter Hull suffered cuts and concussion when he fell heavily.

A crowd far in excess of the reputed 42,000 capacity swelled the stands and terraces for the England and Australia Test match. England won 'the speedway Ashes' for the first time, by virtue of the 55-41 win. The home side won ten of the sixteen races and a majority of minor places. Australia, once again, had failed to break their Hyde Road 'hoodoo'. Many had travelled by train to Manchester from London (such was the interest in the series) and they were able to return having seen a thrilling and sporting contest.

Wembley returned, on 9 September, to the scene of their shock defeat a few weeks previously for another league match. It was to end as one of the darkest and saddest days in the long history of speedway at Belle Vue. After two races, Manchester were 10-1 in arrears. This was partly down to the accident between 'Indian' Allen and Max Grosskreutz. Heat two had the promise of an excellent race, but very early on, one of the most unfortunate accidents seen at Belle Vue took place.

Max made a great effort to pass Harry Whitfield and George Greenwood on the pit bend, but overslid. He was pitched from the bike and Allen, who was running last, was too close to avoid Max's machine. The 'Indian' landed heavily onto the track and he was gently taken to the ambulance room, suffering rib and, more critically, skull injuries. He was later transferred to the Manchester Royal Infirmary. Some tabloids later reported the story incorrectly, much to the annoyance of EOS and Belle Vue. They made out that it was Max Grosskreutz who had run into Allen and caused the injuries. The meeting was completed without complaint; the loss of one rider can be overcome, but against a crack Wembley side it was too much. Grosskreutz continued in the meeting and won his two remaining outings. The resulting 36-16 defeat came as no surprise to anyone present. The wellbeing of an injured colleague bore far more importance than two league points.

For different reasons, 12 September brought joy and much sorrow, with Leeds visiting in the first leg of the Northern Cup final. Against Belle Vue's strongest team, Leeds was hopelessly outclassed. Frank Varey and Eric Langton both scored maximum points. The final outcome in favour of Belle Vue (37-16) tells its own story. Euphoria soon changed to despair after the interval, when it was announced to a silent crowd that James Allen had lost his fight for life. A two minutes silence was impeccably observed, with 22,000 spectators standing with heads bared. After respects had been paid, the crowd was informed that further racing had been abandoned. On hearing this, a stunned and hushed crowd departed from the stadium.

The 'Indian' may have ridden his last race, however, in the short time he had been at Belle Vue, James Allen had made a host of friends. He was a popular man with riders and fans alike and always looking for ways to improve his track performance. Indian's funeral was held at Stillington, near Middlesbrough. Belle Vue management, officials and riders, including Max Grosskreutz, made the journey. An emblem of sympathy was taken in the form of a floral cushion, bearing a black ace of clubs. Within four months of Allen's death, Belle Vue was to lose two other riders in equally tragic circumstances.

James 'Indian' Allen, who was tragically killed in 1931.

Eric Langton pictured with Frank Varey and a Belle Vue official whose name is not known.

The return leg of the final also formed part of a double-header meeting with Belle Vue. Carrying a 21 point lead into the match was more than enough to see Belle Vue lift the Knockout Trophy. Leeds put up a fighting display and was unlucky to lose by 27-26. Included against Leeds were two former captains, Langton and Charles. Frank Charles had returned to Belle Vue in July, after a short spell at Fullerton Park. In the league match, Leeds turned the tables on Belle Vue, winning by the same margin. A few changes to the Belle Vue team saw Grosskreutz, Charles and Cort replaced by Moore, Woods and Oliver Langton.

A racing committee meeting decided to terminate the contract of the track manager, Bernard Brook. The decision for the dismissal was taken on 10 October and under the terms of his agreement Brook would receive three months' pay in lieu. The termination was later altered by a week, due to the extension of the racing season.

Frank Varey proved his versatility by playing a football match for Manchester Central, who played their home games at Hyde Road. Frank made his bow in a Manchester League match against McMahons. Arthur Franklyn was selected to ride in the Southern League Captains' Championship that was held at Wimbledon. Arthur gained a single win and three second places, a total of nine points.

During October, at a meeting of the committee, EOS spoke of his desire to start a Belle Vue Speedway Supporters' Club. He felt that the time was right for a properly organised club. In the past, they had flirted with the idea, but nothing had ever happened.

The close season brought yet more sad news to Belle Vue. Bruce McCallum, a young Australian rider who had come to Hyde Road in 1930, died at Withington Hospital after

Walter Norbury Hull.

a painful illness. It was brought to Belle Vue's attention that the young man was to be buried in a pauper's grave. The management would not allow this to happen and agreed unanimously to pay all of McCallum's funeral expenses. Bruce was buried on 18 November 1931.

Walter Norbury Hull was the most improved rider and he really made his mark in 1931. Walter was born in Hale, Cheshire, in 1907 and rode in the early Audenshaw meetings. He used a variety of machinery from Douglas to Norton. That first meeting at Audenshaw earned young Walter £5 – not bad for a novice! However, when he took part in a second event and came away with £15 in prize money, he realised that this was a good way to make money.

Hull's next stop was the White City, Manchester, where he became a roaring success and gained many titles to his name. Hull had been using a Rudge machine at the White City and found that it did not suit his style, so he returned to a Douglas. The closure of White City in July 1930 saw Hull's allegiances move over the city to Hyde Road and it was here that he made the rapid progress in the Northern League team. At this time, Hull also experimented with the construction of his own frames; they became known around Belle Vue as 'Wally's Camel'.

Everyone was aware that some noted riders had been riding at the blacklisted Audenshaw Speedway in 1931. EOS received a letter from a supporter alleging that he was sure that he had seen contracted Belle Vue riders, Len Woods and Ernest Young, riding there. The matter was investigated but taken no further.

The now annual migration to South America by the Belle Vue boys commenced when Varey took a team over to ride at Montevideo, Uruguay. Initially, Frank was supposedly staying in England to rest during the close season. Others who took the trip were Bob Harrison, Clem Cort, the Langtons and Alan Jeffries (who was Frank's mechanical aid). Oliver Langton and Clem Cort also took their wives on the trip.

The tour was to prove an eventful one, where nothing went to plan. Tragedy was to cast a dark cloud over the boys who were encountering problems of their own.

1932

Speedway in Uruguay was not run on the same lines as in England and soon the money dried up as the promotions went bust. Frank Varey and Eric Langton secretly sailed across the River Plate to see what was happening in Buenos Aires. It was essential that some bookings were found. All the riders were literally broke and desperate for some income.

As the pair was returning from Montevideo, they heard that Clem Cort had been seriously injured in a motorcycle accident. It appeared that Harrison, Cort and Oliver Langton had been going back to their hotel to prepare for the departure to Buenos Aires. All three were on one bike when a car, with no lights on, came from nowhere and hit the riders. Clem was rushed to hospital, critically injured, and he died the following morning.

Although the boys were low on funds, they managed to find enough to pay for a grave for Clem, who had to be buried quickly. The group was due to flee the country on the midnight boat and Harrison was being held in jail for his part in the crash, by innocently saying he was the one in control of the bike. Against the odds, they managed to free Bob on bail with what money remained. Bikes and belongings were removed from within the stadium and transported to the boat in secrecy. All of the riders were under contract to Montevideo Speedway and breaking this could cause further problems.

A distressed Mrs Cort wished to travel with them – not only had she lost her husband but she too had no money. The troupe held a charity meeting, with everything earned being donated to her. Money was of the essence to them, however, that paled into insignificance in the circumstances. The memory of a dear comrade and the needs of his widow came first.

One incident Varey loved to tell at supporters' functions happened on this trip and was verified by Alan Morrey, clerk of the course at Belle Vue and a close associate of Frank down the years. Frank had telegraphed EOS to ask for assistance to get everyone home in time for the English season. After deliberation, EOS telegraphed back and told Varey to 'Swim!'

Weather conditions in Argentina were no different to England – how it rained! Consequently, precious little money came their way and it was only after desperate talks that the Argentine promoters agreed to pay their fares home.

Before the English season started, increases in riders' pay rates were officially announced on 9 February. Appearance money was abolished and promoters would pay all the money won by teams, for home or away inter-track matches. National League matches would be 15s (75p) per start, 15s (75p) per point, with a guarantee of £3. A rate of £1 would apply to cup matches, with a guarantee of £5. For the final, point money would increase to 30s (£1.50). For Test matches the rates would be 30s (£1.50) per start, plus £2 per point.

Flying had, for a long time, been close to the heart of Belle Vue stalwart Arthur Franklyn. He possessed a professional flying licence and was a regular competitor in the

King's Cup race. He had been forced down near Nottingham, when the last race was held. During the close season, Franklyn was offered a commission in the Royal Air Force. At his own request, Arthur asked to not be considered for racing in 1932 and, at the same time, announced his retirement from speedway.

In previous seasons, some visiting team managers had expected access to the centre green as their right. EOS did not view the situation this way and defined the role of any visiting team manager himself. During the 1932 season, team managers had to conduct their duties from within the pit area. Only with the permission of the clerk of the course could any manager be allowed to leave the pit area. A new set of passes was to be issued to help police this situation. All previous passes would be rendered obsolete, as would any ACU badges that had, in the past, allowed access to the pit area.

Many supporters were unhappy that any changes to the race line-up were not announced, in some cases, until after the race was completed. EOS decreed that all substitutions were to be announced prior to a race starting. The boss was also in favour of copies of the rulebook being made available to the general public.

EOS was less than happy with the dress code of certain officials and staff. If the club provided a uniform for race nights, then it was to be worn on duty. For anyone doubting this, he made it quite clear that the situation would not be tolerated. The salaries for race nights were to remain as they had been in 1931.

Over the winter period, many alterations to the stadium and racing facilities had taken place. Never being one to rest on his laurels, EOS invested money on improving an already thriving business. His was a correct way of thinking, as opposed to the 'get rich quick' promoters from the past.

Gone was the old wire fence; riders would now be faced with a white board safety fence. By installing this, a bigger crowd could be accommodated and given a clearer view of the riders against the white background. EOS joked that Billy could now live up to his name of 'Ride the Fence' Lamont. The stadium too had been given a lick of paint for the new season.

The race surface had a completely new look to it. Reg West, the Australian, had assisted with the preparation. For the first time, it did not consist completely of cinders – granite and cinders were mixed together to give a finer, but grippier top surface.

A new location for the steward's box had to be found; the ACU requirement was that this must now be inside the race circuit. This was sited opposite the main stand. Switches for the perimeter lights were relocated in the box.

In 1932, there was only to be one National League, instead of the north and south sections of the previous year. This year would be run in two sections – the first being a preliminary one. The idea was that after this first part had been completed, some teams would drop out and leave the best to fight it out for the league championship, although this did not happen in the end.

The nucleus of riders for 1932 at Belle Vue were Frank Varey, Max Grosskreutz, 'Dusty' Haigh, Eric Langton, Fred Strecker, Frank Charles, Walter Hull, 'Chun' Moore, Eric Gregory, Harold Hastings, Bob Harrison and Larry Boulton. Harold Hastings' move to Belle Vue was hastened by the decision of Lea Bridge to adopt betting on racing. This

Belle Vue, 1932. From left to right, back row: Eric Gregory, Broncho Dixon, Max Grosskreutz, Frank Varey, Len Woods, Oliver Langton, Harold Hastings, Frank Charles. Front row: Joe Abbott, Larry Boulton, Eric Langton, 'Dusty' Haigh, Bob Harrison.

resulted in them being excluded from the National Speedway Association and they were overlooked for the league racing.

Another newcomer was to have been Joe Abbott, the ex-Preston rider. Poor Joe had to miss a chunk of the season through illness and a road accident. He had sustained a fractured skull and leg injuries as a result of the crash. Abbott's condition was critical for some time after the accident. At one stage during his absence, Abbott announced his retirement from speedway – he wanted to concentrate on his garage business. It did not take too long, however, for Joe to rescind his decision.

The doors opened on another season, full of expectations, on 26 March and, this year, there would be no easy matches, as there had been in the Northern League. Tributes were written for Clem Cort and Bruce McCallum in the *Belle Vue Bulletin*. This was the first opportunity the club and spectators had to pay their respects.

Stamford Bridge opened part one of the league programme and left the Hyde Road faithful stunned. The 'Bridge' simply rode their luck, as Belle Vue stumbled from one problem to another. A catastrophic series of falls, motor failures and disqualifications presented the visitors with a 28-24 win and two shock points. For Stamford Bridge, Dicky Smythe achieved the rare feat of remaining unbeaten in his three rides at Belle Vue. Jack Chapman would have been unbeaten, had the toe of his boot not come off when leading the field.

Four days later, Sheffield bore the brunt of the backlash, when the rampant Lancastrians routed the Yorkshiremen 37-15 at Owlerton, much to the delight of EOS. Southampton suffered a similar fate as the rich vein of form continued. Sheffield arrived looking to repair the damage inflicted ten days earlier and, to their credit, achieved a much better performance. The early heats were evenly contested up to heat six, before the home side gradually eased away. An injury to Varey caused alarm in the home camp. He and Langton had collided close to the finish line, when Varey's engine seized up. The fans' favourite was carried off unconscious. Twenty minutes had elapsed before Varey regained his senses, with nothing more than slight concussion.

At Belle Vue, Max Grosskreutz rode his home leg of the British Individual Championship, little short of an invalid. At Sheffield, Max had broken his jaw, but the doctor would only allow him to ride in the one event – he was withdrawn from the league clash. Not only did he beat Arthur Jervis 2-1, but he also managed to establish a track record of 77.8 seconds.

In 1931, the British Individual Speedway Championship had eluded Eric Langton when he was so close to contesting the final. Eric's quest for individual glory began at Belle Vue in April. Belle Vue was represented by Langton and Max Grosskreutz, the results were as follows:

First Round

16 April	Belle Vue	1st Leg	D. Case beat E. Langton	2-1
25 April	Wimbledon	2nd Leg	E. Langton beat D. Case	2-0
5 May	Wembley	Decider	E. Langton beat D. Case	2-0
23 April	Belle Vue	1st Leg	M. Grosskreutz beat A. Jervis	2-1
26 April	West Ham	2nd Leg	M. Grosskreutz beat A. Jervis	2-0

Second Round

21 May	Belle Vue	1st Leg	E. Langton beat M. Grosskreutz	2-0
28 May	Belle Vue	2nd Leg	M. Grosskreutz beat E. Langton	2-0
18 June	Belle Vue	Decider	E. Langton beat M. Grosskreutz	2-1

Semi Final

17 Aug	Stamford Bridge	1st Leg	E. Langton beat F. Arthur	2-0
7 Sept	Belle Vue	2nd Leg	Cancelled	

Frank Arthur injured his knee and was unable to contest the second leg. Langton was given a bye to the final.

Final

24 Sept	Belle Vue	1st Leg	E. Langton beat J. Parker	3-0
5 Oct	Clapton	2nd Leg	Cancelled	

Jack Parker fractured his collarbone at Belle Vue and was unable to continue in the final. The title was, therefore, awarded to Eric Langton.

The riders found themselves a new club mascot, when Len Woods found a black cat with a paw in splints. Woods had noticed the cat limping across the track and went to pick it up. A first aid man attended to the broken paw. Now that Johnnie the bulldog had gone, the riders adopted the lucky black cat and named it 'Speedway'.

West Ham gave a tame performance on the last day of April – more had been expected of them. The match with Wembley loomed on the horizon and was eagerly anticipated by everyone. Belle Vue were not expecting anything less than the hardest match yet. The publicity moguls went into action to build up the clash, which was advertised as the 'The Cock of the North' *v.* 'The Pride of the South' and was the first encounter between the northern and southern champions of 1931. Over 32,000 packed the stands and terraces, including a party of over 200 from Wembley, to cheer their heroes.

After four races, the teams were level at 12 apiece. Wembley then silenced the crowd by taking a shock lead. Haigh and Lees clashed at the start and around the first turn. Lees felt the wrath from a section of fans for his actions – unjustly in most people's eyes. Certainly Haigh saw no reason to remonstrate with Lees' hard racing was only to be expected. Rumours spread that 'Dusty' had given 'Ginger' a black eye – nothing could have been further from the truth.

A pulsating match stood at 21-21 with seven races gone. The crowd went wild as the Varey/Langton pairing decided the outcome with some tenacious teamwork. In the final race, George Greenwood shot away from the start with Charles and Grosskreutz making no attempt to race him. A shared heat left the final score 29-25 in favour of Belle Vue. Harold Hastings had ridden all night with the handicap of an ankle injury, his 3 points proving vital to the outcome. The 2 welcome match points lifted Belle Vue to the top of the tree. Erratic away form was to stop the Belle Vue charge up the league table in the coming weeks.

Frank Charles' form was a concern to the management and supporters. Calls were made for him to be replaced by one of the 'squad riders', who, as yet, had not ridden in the team. Frank's form had literally disappeared and his bikes were simply not fast enough. Later in the season, Charles retired, following an injury to his good friend, Joe Abbott, who was also his riding partner. With Len Woods, 'Chun' Moore, Walter Hull and Oliver Langton awaiting the call to action, EOS and Harris had a choice of replacements. At other clubs, any of these four would have automatically made the side.

Plymouth travelled to Manchester on a run of poor returns and this continued in an uneven contest. An effortless 36-18 win kept up the challenge to the main contenders. The 5-match unbeaten run ended in controversial circumstances at West Ham and highlighted flaws in the Belle Vue armoury.

Belle Vue were dissatisfied with the condition of the track and Varey contended that it was bumpy. However, the track was not the only problem for Frank. He was unhappy with the starting procedure and offered to concede the match to West Ham, which was refuted by the steward. Events in the seventh race lit the blue touch paper, when Varey and Langton deliberately held back on the start line. Frank flew from the start, infuriating the crowd, which was not slow to vent its anger at the pair. On their way to the dressing room, the Belle Vue lads had to walk a gauntlet of hatred. Here they found a venomous mob waiting for them. Varey was spat at and, predictably, he retaliated, by giving the offending supporter, in his own words, 'a couple of lessons'. The police had to intervene and quell the warring factions. The match was a non-event and the 34-20 defeat was a bitter blow after such a fine start.

Joe Abbott.

It was then announced to an amazed crowd that Belle Vue were refusing to ride in the second-half scratch races. A complaint had been lodged about Tommy Croombs' engine allegedly being 'oversized'. Tommy's bike was taken for measuring and pronounced legal for racing. A report was filed with the ACU concerning the events of the night. Belle Vue had to be smuggled out of the stadium to escape further trouble.

Frank Varey and Oliver Langton were both down to attempt to reach 100 mph at Brooklands – they both wanted the gold star that was awarded to anyone achieving this. It was thought that a properly geared-up speedway machine could do speeds of between 105 and 110 mph. The tremendously speedy machines worked harder at 40 mph than they would at 100 mph.

Southampton were the next to try their luck in Manchester. A poor showing by them permitted Belle Vue to coast home. They dropped only three points to Southampton in a one-sided match to record what was, at that time, their best home win (42-12). The unbeaten sequence continued with home and away wins against Coventry. At Belle Vue, Coventry fared worse than Southampton and went down by 43-10. Surprisingly, when they visited Plymouth, at Pennycross, Belle Vue struggled to cope with the stout riding home team and scraped a 3-point win.

All good things come to an end and this was no exception. The vital trips to Wimbledon and Wembley, in a four-day period, would make or break any title aspirations – and so it proved to be. At Plough Lane, Belle Vue had themselves to blame for a cruel defeat. In a disastrous fourth race, Langton had a rare fall, but worse was to come when Varey followed suit. This 6-point lead was a gift to Wimbledon – and it was a lead that they would not relinquish. Walter Hull, making his 1932 debut, pleased everyone by top-scoring with 7 points. After the main match, a team of Australians, 'The Kangaroos', beat Belle Vue in a four-a-side challenge match. The Australians had an easy win by 15-9.

The show moved to the Empire Stadium on Thursday for the most important match to date. Wembley were pushing in the upper reaches of the division, and a win over Belle Vue was vital to keep the charge going. A narrow defeat, by 28-25, effectively ended any lingering thoughts of Belle Vue finishing at the top.

An ACU inquiry delayed the hearing to hand out the punishments from the Belle Vue walkout at West Ham. The reason for the delay was caused by the two riders in question, Varey and Langton, not being available to give evidence. Until this happened, the proposed sentences could not be imposed. Pending the appeal, the sentences were that Varey was to be fined £5 and Langton £3. Other team members were to have £1 fines given. Jack Harris, the team manager, was to receive a severe reprimand.

Wimbledon arrived at Belle Vue in high spirits, only to come up against a revenge-seeking side. From the outset, Wimbledon were torn apart, the 35-18 scoreline partly making up for the narrow loss in London. A surprise home defeat came the following week, when Crystal Palace deservedly went home with the points. One week later, Belle Vue had a terrible time in the return match and went down 34-18.

Seven days later, they were back in London once more. On this trip, the team had a good travelling support. Over 600 supporters were taken to Stamford Bridge on the first-ever specially chartered train from Piccadilly Station. Beforehand, they had decorated the carriages with black and red streamers – the engine itself bore the club emblem, the Ace of Clubs.

Winning the preliminary section may have been a distant thought. However, it did not stop Belle Vue from giving Stamford Bridge a big scare. After four races, Belle Vue led by 6 points, only for 'The Bridge' to hit back with three successive maximum heat advantages. A late fightback was not enough to prevent Stamford Bridge from retaining an unbeaten home record, with a 29-25 win. Varey topped the scorechart with 6 points, but Stamford Bridge had three riders who only dropped a single point between them. A train packed with weary supporters arrived back in Manchester at 5 a.m., tired but pleased with the efforts of the team in the first half of the season.

Having completed the fixtures for the National League matches, Belle Vue held a commendable fourth place. At least the team had an idea of the task that lay ahead in the battle for the National League Championship. Coventry was the opposition for the opening National League Championship match. Previously, Belle Vue had little trouble in overcoming Coventry and perhaps entered this match feeling too confident. Losing by $32\frac{1}{2}$-$21\frac{1}{2}$ was not the start they had anticipated – if the team was to make a serious challenge, there could be no more results like this.

At Plymouth, all the team seemed lacking in form and only retained the slender lead by putting up a fight. In race three, after two Plymouth lads had fallen, the ACU steward made an unbelievable decision. Harrison and Langton crossed the finish line in that order, only to find out that Harrison was to be disqualified, having been deemed guilty of foul riding. Langton, now the only finisher, was only awarded two points for his second place behind Harrison. Although this had no direct effect on the result, the ACU decided that Langton should have received the 3 points for his win. In doing this, the score was amended from 24-23 to 25-23 in Belle Vue's favour.

Frank Varey was top-scorer with 8 points and both Frank and Langton scored 11 of the teams' 24 points. It was surprising that the pair did so well. The team was due to leave en bloc for Devon, on the 9.25 a.m. train from London Road (Piccadilly). Varey and Langton had not arrived by the departure time and were left behind. Unbeknown to anyone on the train, Frank and the Langton brothers had set off from Leeds at 8.20 a.m., only to be held up by a bank of fog on the moors. After loading their bikes onto a trailer at the stadium, they arrived at the station 10 minutes after the train had left. The trio decided to drive to Crewe in an attempt to catch up with the train. Further misfortune happened when they had tyre trouble. After this setback their only option was to drive the 300 miles to Plymouth and hope to arrive in time – which was a tall order, given the lack of fast roads in 1932! Langton's 'racing' Bugatti was driven non-stop to Plymouth. Surprisingly, the journey was completed at 5.35 p.m., one hour *before* the train was due in – which must have been a great relief to their team-mates and travelling officials.

Sandwiched between the two matches was the Test match at Belle Vue. Winning at Hyde Road was not something Australia seemed particularly adept at and the 1932 meeting was no different. Before racing commenced, the 'Kangaroos' were dealt a double blow. Star man, Ron Johnson, broke down en route to Manchester and Dicky Smythe was involved in a car crash. Dicky eventually arrived and took what would have been his third ride, but that was the end of his night's racing.

Parker and Langton gave the Lions a great start in heat one. Huxley bolted from the start line with the two Lions on his tail. Realising Vic was taking him wide, Langton cleverly held back and allowed Parker to pass the Australian, with a tremendous burst of speed on the inside line. Langton had, by now, cut back and nipped over the line ahead of Huxley. This was certainly one of the most talked about races over the years. At the interval, England led 26-22 and, in the second half, the Lions were firing on all cylinders. The trio of Parker, Varey and Lees lost a point apiece to the Aussies; they alone provided the platform for a superb 58-43 English victory which was enjoyed by 42,000 jubilant supporters.

In the *Daily Mail* National Trophy, West Ham had been drawn as Belle Vue's first opponents. Eight-man teams were called for in this competition. EOS had not enjoyed their early exit in 1931 at the hands of Wimbledon. Success in the trophy was a realistic aim, whereas expecting to claim the league championship was perhaps a little premature. Long-time absentee Joe Abbott had, apparently, fully recovered from his accident and car crash injuries, to reclaim his place in the line-up. Varey and Abbott gave the perfect start with a maximum win, which was equalled by Haigh and Gregory in the next race. Belle Vue could not have expected a 10-2 lead after two races – it was a dream start. West Ham did not know what had hit them and, by the halfway stage, were 18 points in arrears. Not even the incomparable 'Bluey' Wilkinson could stem the onslaught, with Arthur Atkinson being the most effective visitor. After the interval the match continued in very much the same vein, although West Ham fared slightly better overall. Perhaps the most telling statistic was that out of sixteen races, West Ham managed only two heat advantages. The final scoreline of 64-32 provided Belle Vue with a vital cushion for the second leg three nights later, on 26 July.

Joe Abbott had given a terrific performance and his new partnership with Frank Varey was working out very well. Joe had notched a creditable return of 7 points from four rides and it was only after the meeting that Joe made a startling revelation: he should not really have ridden! Abbott had taken part against the wishes of his doctor, while still having a crack in his skull from his car crash many months before.

In July, two riders bade farewell to Hyde Road. 'Chun' Moore transferred to Clapton, for a fee of £75 on the 8th. Later, on 24th, Walter Hull joined the London exodus, when he departed to Wimbledon. The return clash of the *Daily Mail* Trophy caused few problems for Belle Vue. West Ham won the tie with ease, with Belle Vue merely defending their 32-point lead. Although West Ham threatened at times, it proved too much, with Belle Vue winning the tie by an overall aggregate score of 106-83.

A popular theory was going round that Belle Vue was beaten before they arrived at London tracks. To some degree this may have been true, but the team never gave less than maximum effort: EOS would not allow slackness. On 6 August, the Fourth Test match was being held at Crystal Palace, with Belle Vue riders involved. Despite this, Belle Vue held a meeting and welcomed back some old favourites for a night of 'Old Time Stars'. The 25,000 who attended had many memories revived. The programmed riders would have done any early meetings proud. Among those attending were:

A.B. Drew
Rex Kirby – 'Big Elbows'
Alec McLachlan
Cyril Wilcock
'Ham' Burrill
Fred Fearnley
Jack Wood

'Dank' Ewan – Belle Vue's 'India Rubber Man'
'Acorn' Dobson
George Milton
Charlie Bentley
Larry Coffey
Dick Hayman

'Skid' Skinner could not accept the invitation as he was putting on a Wall-of-Death Show in Poland. Jack Wood appeared riding his Douglas and fully masked. Drew wore his famous multi-coloured jersey from his White City days. Most of the riders were out of condition, except for Wilcock and Coffey, who compared favourably with the current riders of the day. The Old Time Stars Final was won by Cyril Wilcock in 89.6 seconds, which was only six seconds slower than Grosskreutz's record. Eric Gregory had a magnificent ride to win the Supporters' Trophy. Having been left hopelessly at the start, Gregory, with some daring cornering, overcame his rivals in style. Having been unable to ride through injuries until early June, Abbott ended up on the casualty list again. Poor Joe was having a wretched season, having just re-established himself in the side. In fact, he could consider himself lucky to have escaped a far more serious injury during the pile-up. A badly gashed hand required thirty stitches and a few weeks on the other side of the fence.

Belle Vue's league form was fine – four straight wins put Belle Vue second behind Wembley. The London jinx raised its head again when Wimbledon ended the run with a single point win at Plough Lane. For the first time ever, a drawn match occurred at Belle Vue. Wimbledon tied at 26 apiece, inflicting further damage to any championship notions the club had. Wimbledon rode a hard, but fair match and fully deserved the one league point gained. Grosskreutz had a lucky escape when he fell in the eighth race. Dicky Case, who was in close pursuit, ran over Max's leg. Both Case and the machine were flung into the air, with Case hitting the fence still seated on his bike. Miraculously, Case retained control and crossed the winning line first. The visitors rode with five riders only for the first six heats. Claude Rye and Con Cantrell arrived late at the track and were only able to take their last rides. Belle Vue's 'terrible twins', Varey and Langton, were accepting any bookings they could possibly find in order to adapt to the southern circuits. They and the club were desperate to find a way to lay the London bogey.

At this time, Belle Vue had what they termed 'better priced seats' and the demand for these was three times greater than previously. Lord Stanley, who was the Earl of Derby's son, had become a frequent visitor to Belle Vue. Speedway was now attracting a better class of spectator than it had done in the past. Well-heeled families from Lancashire and Cheshire were also prominent at meetings.

The Star Championship meeting to decide on a representative was held on 20 August. The supporters were asked to vote for a second representative by completing a slip inside the programme. Both riders would go forward to the Wembley Final. Lord Stanley of Alderley attended the meeting and was seated in the 'Royal box', which was

'Broncho' Dixon.

reserved for distinguished visitors. Langton won the meeting, with Frank Varey being the rider afforded most votes by the public. Langton received his Bronze Star from Lord Stanley in front of 25,000 cheering fans.

The visit of Plymouth was a non-event and they were lucky to escape with the 35-15 defeat. Falls and machine troubles for Belle Vue saved Plymouth from a heavier loss. Three days earlier, a trip to Stamford Bridge stretched the sequence of losses in London, when Belle Vue lost 30-22. Worse was to come when Belle Vue were 'taken to the cleaners' by Wembley, at the Empire Stadium. The 41-13 shambles was, by far, the worst display of the season, yet, to be fair, Wembley possessed a star-studded line-up, capable of overcoming any team. In the return match a couple of days later, Belle Vue managed a win, but only just.

September arrived with championship aspirations now all but a distant memory. However, there was the small matter of cup glory in the offing. Belle Vue had a league victory over Stamford Bridge and an away loss at West Ham on either side of the first leg. The semi-final first leg at Wimbledon fell foul of the weather, making the home leg crucial to the final outcome. Any worries subsided, with Belle Vue taking a 19-point lead to Plough Lane. Grosskreutz and Langton had each shown their best form, with both recording four wins apiece. A resounding home win over West Ham sent the team to Wimbledon in good heart – and it showed. Defending their lead, Belle Vue had the misfortune to lose skipper, Frank Varey, after two races. Riding with his usual panache, Frank walloped the fence and demolished a section of it. After collapsing, Varey was stretchered off and was unable to take his remaining outings. Langton and Dixon were Belle Vue's best pair, with 17 points, in the 50-46 defeat. A dream final with Wembley now loomed, but could Belle Vue give a good performance at Wembley – something they had to achieve to give a realistic chance of winning the cup?

League form suggested that the team was riding well, and the visit of Clapton presented few problems, with Belle Vue running out 38-16 victors. The misfortunes of Joe Abbott continued. Poor Joe had been injured prior to the season's start and was injured again just after his comeback. Now, he suffered more bad luck when a fire destroyed his garage, car and two motorcycles – he lost £600 as a result.

Two nights previously, Eric Langton had his greatest success to date. He won the £100 first prize and the Silver Star at the Star Championship final at Wembley. Dicky Case had beaten Langton in the semi-final, but Eric qualified as the fastest second-placed rider. Although drawn on the outside start, Langton swooped round his rivals on the first lap and pulled away for a comfortable win.

On the eve of the Wembley leg of the final, Belle Vue entertained a team of Australian riders, who raced as a team called the 'Kangaroos' in a six-a-side challenge. Appalling weather rendered the track a mud heap and, with the final only twenty-four hours away, no home rider would take unnecessary risks. The 'Kangaroos' won the day by 29-20, when perhaps proceedings should not have taken place. The rain was so bad that the post-interval heats were abandoned. Times had been around the 95-second mark, which was 21 seconds slower than the 4-lap record.

Belle Vue may have arrived in good spirits and form, but they left devastated by a sound 66-29 beating at the hands of Wembley. EOS was the first to admit that there

Joe Abbott, Larry Boulton and Max Grosskreutz.

were no excuses, his team was outridden. Varey was handed a disqualification for jumping the start, in a sensational beginning to the meeting, as was Langton in the last race. Eric Gregory proved the most consistent rider for Belle Vue.

The return, on 15 October, at Hyde Road, was merely a formality for the rampant Lions. Try as they did, Belle Vue was in a hopeless situation to retrieve a deficit of 37 points. The home team won by 58-37, but failed on aggregate by 103-87. At the halfway stage, the scores were tied at 24 each, but in the second half Belle Vue turned on the style and threw caution to the wind. On a wet track, falls were frequent and Haigh and Dixon took tumbles when positioned well. In this half, Belle Vue grabbed 34 of the 40 points available One interesting point regarding the two teams was that Wembley had one Londoner, Colin Watson, and Belle Vue had one Lancastrian, Joe Abbott.

Belle Vue's home season was wrapped up on 19 October with a challenge against a team of London riders. The one outstanding league fixture at Crystal Palace was the last outing for Belle Vue in 1932. A 30-24 loss left Belle Vue in a creditable third place. Most of the southern-based teams now realised that they did have a serious threat in the Belle Vue team. If there was a need for improvement, it would have to be on the away circuits. Although nobody knew it at the time, there were exciting times ahead for the club, who were to dominate domestic matters.

1933

Over the winter period, work was done on improving the look of an already impressive stadium. The track had been given more banking to make cornering safer. However, EOS's burning desire was to secure the championship pennant. To hasten the process, winter training schools were held in an attempt to find new blood. From these, Belle Vue unearthed three riders who showed natural ability. Henry Walker, Fred Tate and William Kitchen stood out against all other aspiring trainees and were earmarked for second-half races. Walker and Tate were both genuine discoveries, but Kitchen did have a reasonable background to racing. He had a lot of experience on the grass tracks in the north and had also raced the speedways, on and off, from 1929. Bill had ridden at Barrow (Little Park), Workington (Lonsdale Park), Burnley and Preston. And now he wanted to finally make a name for himself as a star speedway rider. Work at the family garage in Galgate, Lancaster, had prevented Bill from entering racing much earlier.

For the first time, at a cost of £3 10s (£3.50), Belle Vue made it possible to purchase a season ticket. This would guarantee a seat for every league and cup match. Representative match tickets would still have to be applied for. In addition, patrons could also reserve a parking spot at the stadium for a further 10s (50p). Rules and regu-

Junior rider Henry Walker.

lations also played a big part in the early season make up of the side. It was decreed that no team could retain more than nine riders – that could explain the absence of Grosskreutz during April and May. Initially, Max had received an offer to ride the season in Hamburg, Germany, and had decided to accept it. He did, however, travel to Manchester to meet up with EOS. Grosskreutz made it clear that if he rode again in England, it would only be with Belle Vue. The wily EOS suspected that Max would be back soon – and he was correct.

The nine riders retained by the club were: Frank Varey, Eric Langton, Joe Abbott, 'Broncho' Dixon, Eric Gregory, Bob Harrison, Larry Boulton, Oliver Langton and 'Dusty' Haigh. However, within a month, Haigh had returned to Sheffield, with Henry Walker also

Overnight sensation – Bill Kitchen.

making the weekly trip over the Woodhead Pass. Fred Tate and Fred Strecker were both transferred to Nottingham to help strengthen the side. Bill Kitchen took the place of Haigh. Oliver Langton, although listed as retained, only rode when he was needed. The club hardly missed Grosskreutz – Kitchen was an overnight sensation, surprising many with the ease in which he settled into the harsh world of league racing.

Another new innovation was the starting gate, invented by Crystal Palace promoter, Fred Mockford. At last, something to make starts less irritating and to prevent Varey from false starting. A big change for Manchester Speedway was the status of the riders; Frank Varey was asked to distribute trophies at the NMMC dinner. More importantly, they were requested to open a motor show at Paulden's Store in Manchester (now known as Debenhams). During the following years, the riders' services were wanted even more, as their fame increased.

The season began on 15 April with a series of open events, but the league did not start until May. Eric Langton was due back from New Zealand in time to ride on 29 April, in a league selection match. Varey and Gregory, both injured, could not take part in this match, but EOS had already decided on the opening line-up. Kitchen made a sensational start by winning his three rides and, earlier in the day, had won the *Daily Dispatch* 100 miles race on the sands at Southport.

Eric Langton sprang a surprise on Belle Vue by announcing that he would not ride in the opening league match, on 6 May – he regarded this as his unlucky day. Seven years previously, Eric was badly injured in a road accident. A year later, Oliver, his brother, broke a wrist. Eric was due to ride at Glasgow in 1929, on 6 May, but he decided not to go and a rider was killed at the meeting, hence his reluctance to race on that day.

The league opened with Wimbledon coming north and came close to a shock result. Difficulty in raising a full team gave the Dons problems, therefore the control board gave permission for the temporary loan of Ivor Hill and Jack Chapman. Varey, riding against doctor's orders, took to the track – this was remarkable, as Frank was literally riding one-armed. His injured shoulder was strapped in position and he guided the bike with his one good arm. After two home wins and two away losses (one notably at Wembley), Belle Vue settled into mid-table.

An aerial view of the Great Speedway.

Eric Langton clashed with the ACU over the defence of the British Individual Championship. The ACU noticed that he had not ridden on 6 May, nor had he signed a contract. EOS received the directive that Langton would have to defend the title at Crystal Palace on 20 May. After careful thought, Eric declined to defend the title, as this would deny Belle Vue of his services for the home match against Plymouth. He contended that, as champion, he should defend it on his own track and not handicap his team. 'Why should I travel a few hundred miles to convince people in authority that I am the champion?' he proclaimed. EOS described his action as 'most sporting and unselfish'. As a result, he also forfeited the £5 per week payment to the champion.

Four days later, Frank Varey spoke on behalf of the riders and announced that no members of the Manchester club would compete for the British title. 'A decision by a sportsman,' Varey declared, in praise of Langton. Frank had found trouble during the match at Wembley. At the time it was alleged that he struck 'Ginger' Lees. The control board fined him £5 for the incident and gave him a severe reprimand.

Things began to look up with a home win over Plymouth and a commendable victory at Wimbledon, where Kitchen was only defeated by Vic Huxley. However, everything went wrong when Clapton came to town. Led by Norman and Jack Parker, Clapton gave all teams hope by defeating Belle Vue 36-27 on their own backyard. Only Varey, with 10 points, and 6 from Dixon kept the side afloat. Clapton's success did not please EOS at all and similar performances would severely dent the club's championship hopes. For their part, the riders responded well and reeled off three consecutive home wins over West Ham, Wembley and Crystal Palace. Further success at Sheffield was added before the run ended at Crystal Palace. In the home match against Crystal Palace, visitor Ron Johnson ran into Kitchen's back wheel and was fortunate to escape with a badly sprained thumb. After this, the match went downhill and resulted in a 45-14 win to Belle Vue. A crowd demonstration at the disqualification of Tom Farndon by Bill Campbell, the starter, provoked ill feeling. Farndon was a popular visitor to Hyde Road and the crowd made their feelings known. In the final, Harrison and Langton were dealt with in the same way as Farndon, which only served to increase the tension. Kitchen and Abbott remained to contest the Silver Wheel and the farce was completed when Abbott fell, leaving Kitchen to finish alone.

Clapton, after a bright start, were hit by a run of injuries, which allowed Belle Vue, West Ham and Wimbledon to come back into contention. Seeing the challenge disintegrate prompted them to grumble in the press about their plight. Predictably, EOS picked up on this and made his thoughts known to anyone prepared to listen. All teams had the chance to strengthen, but Clapton considered they were getting a raw deal with regards to riders. They contended that because of the injuries, preference should be given to them over other clubs. Wimbledon took the opportunity to reinforce by signing Wal Phillips and now they had the look of possible champions. In his opinion, EOS thought that clubs should look after their own interests and not bemoan others' attempts to better themselves.

Ex-rider Max Grosskreutz had chosen to ride in Hamburg and, in June, Max was to bring a team of Germans to ride on British tracks. For reasons known only to them, the control board banned the appearance of the Germans. Disappointment was felt in Manchester for Grosskreutz, who was bringing his side (which also included Dicky Case) to race there. The Germans were due to meet a Wembley select side at Belle Vue because the team was on league duty in London. After the ban, the fixture was hastily altered to a challenge match between Sheffield and Wembley. On 16 June, one of the fans' favourite sons returned to the fold. Max immediately went into the side at Nottingham to replace Bill Kitchen. A crushing 41-18 win kept up the challenge for the top spot. Kitchen

Max Grosskreutz.

had been riding in the Isle of Man TT events. Grosskreutz took his home bow in another one-sided match with Coventry, their 46-17 triumph left them in the top position. After the month of May, teams were permitted to add to the nine riders they had elected initially and Max was the ingredient needed to make a good side, a great one.

Belle Vue did compete with a team called 'The Scandinavians' in a four-a-side challenge, winning 23-8. Frank Charles came out of retirement to resume his career in Manchester. He had been persuaded by EOS to help out and he gradually regained something like his expected form. He did find it difficult to break into the team that was now showing championship form. At first, appearances were restricted to cup matches and the odd reserve outing. It was only in the last few months of the season that he regained a regular team spot.

Once again, in the National Trophy, Wimbledon was paired with Belle Vue, in what was now becoming an annual event. Oliver Langton by now was riding very little; he seemed quite content to keep Eric's bikes in good repair. In the Belle Vue pits, Oliver was acknowledged as fine mechanic and definitely the driving force in his brother's success. The word invincible was now well used when referring to Belle Vue. Poor Sheffield had a torrid time and lost 45-18. But for the efforts of Haigh and the recently transferred Larry Boulton, Sheffield's plight would have been far worse. Harrison, Kitchen and Abbott rode unbeaten by any opponent, the win opened up a 4-point lead for Belle Vue over Crystal Palace.

On 1 July in the Star Championship round, the new starting gate (operated by the starter, Bill Campbell) was used for the first time. Varey and Eric Langton progressed to the next phase of the competition. For the forthcoming Test match, Bill Kitchen was only given a reserve spot, when most expected him to be in the side; Varey and Harrison were chosen. The Australians recorded their first win at Belle Vue since the series began in 1930 with a 65-61 victory. The Belle Vue contingent failed to register high scores and only managed 16 points combined.

League duties recommenced with a trip to Devon. At the last attempt, the side suffered an embarrassing loss at Plymouth. Not so this time, as Belle Vue stamped their authority on the proceedings. Wembley arrived with the intent of inflicting defeat on Belle Vue, although they may have been in mid-table, they seemed to reserve good performances for visits to Manchester; the classic meeting that took place enthralled everyone. The old adversaries were locked at 28-28, with one race remaining.

In 'Ginger' Lees and Van Praag, the Lions had an excellent chance of victory, but Langton and Abbott had other ideas. With the crowd in a near hysterical state, Langton turned to Lees and proclaimed, 'I suppose it all depends on me.' Lees shot from the start, as Langton reared violently. For two laps Eric rode the white line, but 'Ginger' held firm. Throwing caution to the wind, Langton swept round the boards and edged past Lees on lap three. He crossed the line to thunderous applause and was chaired by his team-mates back to the start line, with the spectators throwing their hats and programmes into the air. Lees was also given a warm reception for his contribution in this magnificent race.

Perhaps the most important win came at Clapton. Never before had a Belle Vue team won there! This extended the sequence of wins to seven, but this win made the riders

Lionel Van Praag – always difficult to beat at Belle Vue.

feel they now had an excellent chance in the 'big one' against Wimbledon. There was a consensus of opinion that the Dons had a team capable of pushing Belle Vue hard over two legs. EOS was happy to come back to Manchester with a 12-point deficit, but a win would have been better. He even changed the order of riding, showing his regard for the London team. A near capacity crowd at Plough Lane was not disappointed, as both teams provided top-class entertainment. Neither was prepared to give an inch – and every point was fought for. Apart from a third place, Langton won his other rides for his 21 points. He received backing from Kitchen, who claimed 18 points. EOS returned a delighted man after the 64-60 loss that put Belle Vue in the driving seat.

The team steadily drew away from Wimbledon to win 74-51 (134-115 on aggregate) in the second leg. Grosskreutz gave his most accomplished display of the last twelve months, with his maximum 24-point return. His partnership with Bill Kitchen was blossoming and, together, they claimed four maximum heat wins. Frank Charles's recent reappearance at Hyde Road did not guarantee him a place – he was only reserve. The visitors had been handicapped by the loss of Wal Phillips, who had ridden well at Wimbledon but now had a fractured leg. The semi-final draw paired the club with Clapton. As the strength of Belle Vue and Wembley was often being questioned, it became evident that other teams needed to improve to compete with them. For the 1934 season, it was felt that encouragement should be given for all tracks to train their own youngsters.

The Belle Vue machine steamrollered any team blocking their path to the National League Championship. Their unbeaten run, which started on 15 June, continued until

the loss at Clapton on 27 September. The manner of these victories varied: some home matches saw the opposition taken apart – Plymouth lost by 52-11 and Coventry by 50-13 – while the remaining matches were of more reasonable proportions. By overcoming Coventry, the championship was clinched in front of an ecstatic crowd. EOS, however, was a hard taskmaster and he now demanded his team bring the *Daily Mail* National Trophy to Belle Vue.

Messages of congratulations were received from other tracks. Sheffield promoter, Alex Dovener, was delighted that Belle Vue had broken the southern stranglehold on trophies. EOS felt honoured to receive a congratulatory letter from Arthur Elvin, the managing director of Wembley Speedway. Elvin

Joe 'Iron Man' Abbott.

did add that his Lions would be trying to relieve the Manchester club of the silverware in 1934. The *Daily Mail* Trophy was speedway's equivalent of the FA Cup and EOS wanted revenge over Wembley, who beat them in 1932. Clapton stood in the way of the final that everyone wanted. They would have to face Clapton without Bill Kitchen, who was on the injury list. At Clapton, the team gave a solid performance in a match not lacking in incident. In the opening race, Jack Parker fell and broke his leg – the handicap was too much for the home team. Hopes of reaching the final were boosted by the 70-54 win, in which Belle Vue riders won twelve out of the eighteen races.

Already knowing that arch-rivals Wembley were through to the final, the return leg saw Belle Vue in their most devastating form – not one person in the stadium could have predicted the rout by 98-28 (168-82 on aggregate). Grosskreutz recorded 22 points, with the Varey/Langton pairing remaining unbeaten by any Clapton rider. This was a new record cup-tie score at that time. Had Kitchen been fit to ride, who knows what the score might have been!

Exactly what the 400 Clapton fans thought of it, you cannot imagine! To come all the way from London for a non-event must have been disheartening. A Clapton official had the task of giving updates on the meeting to people gathered at the East London track, which must have been difficult. The weakened visitors fought a brave battle against the odds and only Phil Bishop managed to win a race.

On the eve of the away leg of the final, Belle Vue rode at Clapton with a suggestion that other more important matters were in their thoughts. Clapton never looked like losing as the visitors went through the motions. As they were to win all the remaining matches, the club would have stayed undefeated since 17 June, when they had lost at Wimbledon.

Wembley had forever been a daunting arena for Belle Vue teams, who had failed to win a league or cup match at the Empire Stadium. Equally, the Lions realised that they would need a sizeable lead to take with them to Manchester, if they were to stand a realistic chance of retaining the trophy. The tight bends at Wembley had never suited the Belle Vue style, but all this was about to change. Confidence rose immediately when Langton and Varey took full points in the first race. Langton showed the way by equalling the track record and, from that point, Belle Vue rarely looked like being upstaged. For once the usually rampant Lions put on a tame display. The 72-54 loss could partly be attributed to the absent Lees and an ineffective Colin Watson. Only Wally Kilmister, with 18 points, put up any real resistance. Showing a deficit of 11 at the interval, Wembley had further misfortune when Harry Whitfield withdrew from the meeting, after being injured when Abbott ran into him.

Two nights later, Hyde Road was packed to the rafters when a crowd in excess of 42,000 paid admission – this was the biggest attendance since the stadium opened in 1929. A delayed start was necessary to admit the long queues, with many hundreds still locked out. Never had the fans sampled an atmosphere such as this and they were in no doubt that this was to be one of the greatest evenings in Belle Vue's history.

Again, Langton and Varey supplied the perfect start, by taking full points in the opener. They would have remained unbeaten as a pair, had Varey's machine not misbehaved. Wally Kilmister proved a thorn in Belle Vue's side, but he was the only Lion to trouble them. Wembley gave it their best and provided some praiseworthy racing; it was unfortunate for them that the home side was in good form. In several heats, both Wembley riders were in the lead and were picked off by the track-craft of Belle Vue. Varey, with 18 points, top-scored and he received backing from the whole team, with no rider getting fewer than 11 points.

The 92-33 win (164-87 on aggregate) was highly satisfying for EOS, having avenged last year's final defeat. Winning had become a habit and the last four National League matches, all away (at Coventry, Crystal Palace, Wimbledon and again at Wembley), were wins. In the league, the club had a proud record; in the first twelve matches they had just four defeats. The remaining twenty-four yielded a single loss and it was consistency that kept them firmly at the summit. EOS concluded a glorious season on 14 October with a specially arranged challenge between 'The Champions *v.* The Rest'. The Rest, who had a distinct Wembley flavour to them, went down by 44-19. Kitchen, now recovered from a foot injury, simply flew and was aided by Varey and Charles. In the second half, the Supporters' Trophy was won by Kitchen and Varey won the Celebration Trophy in the last race of 1933.

Finally, the team received the *News of the World* Trophy for the league and the *Daily Mail* National Trophy, a richly deserved reward for the hard work undertaken. Some good stories have a bad side to them and this was no exception. Wimbledon manager, Norman Pritchard, penned a column praising Belle Vue, but forewarning them of plans that other promoters were looking at. A daily paper had run a story to the effect that Belle Vue was too strong and should hand over riders. To his credit, Pritchard resisted joining in as Wimbledon had been subjected to similar treatment before the season started. He hoped that EOS would stand firm and ignore this. It was the intention of the Dons to strengthen, so that they could challenge the champions. In any case, he was of the opinion that it was only the 'weak' wanted to take action.

1934

The winter season passed with little activity in Manchester. Belle Vue's stars had been riding in the sunnier climates of the southern hemisphere. Varey, Harrison and the Langton brothers revisited Argentina, while Bill Kitchen took his talents to Australia. They all met with a good deal of success, so much so that Kitchen received an offer to go back at the end of the season. EOS prayed that they would return sharp and ready for the rigours of what he perceived as Belle Vue's toughest test yet. Varey was injured, but was able to make a quick recovery. During the winter break, Eric Gregory and 'Broncho' Dixon were transferred to Wembley. They would have a better chance of having regular racing there.

For the 1934 season, the league comprised of nine clubs, which gave a programme of 32 matches, plus the National Trophy and a new competition, the ACU Cup. Fred Mockford had moved his Crystal Palace side en bloc to New Cross and Clapton were now known as Lea Bridge, even though they still rode at the same stadium. Birmingham came back when the Hall Green track was accepted into the league, but they and Plymouth were to spend the season at the foot of the table.

Belle Vue were to have had a new recruit for the season. An Australian, Arnie Hansen, agreed a deal with them and was all set to come over. At the last minute, Hansen cancelled the arrangement as he had received the offer of a good post as a salesman.

Belle Vue, 1934. From left to right, Frank Varey, Max Grosskreutz, Bob Harrison, Eric Langton, Joe Abbott, Bill Kitchen and Frank Charles, plus team mascot Bob Staye.

Vol. 7. No. 29.
SEPT. 15, 1934.

Issued every Saturday,
6d.

259th MEETING.

BELLE VUE BULLETIN

AND PROGRAMME

All Meetings Under the Auspices of THE NORTH MANCHESTER MOTOR CLUB

BELLE VUE SPEEDWAY

The Management reserve the right to alter or vary this Programme without notice.
Speedway Meeting held under the Speedway Regulations of the Auto-Cycle Union.
Track Licence No. 318.   Permit No. T.A. 705.
The A.C.U. Official Measurement of the Track is 418 yards.
Clerk of the Course, Speedway and Racing Manager : E. O. SPENCE
OFFICIALS :

Steward A.C.U. - A. TAYLOR		Timekeeper (A.C.U. Appointment)
Judge - - - W. H. S. ANDREW		H. S. WHEELDON

Mechanical Superintendent MAURICE GAVSON   Medical Officers - DRS. MILNE & MACLEAN
St. John's Ambulance Brigade in attendance.

W. PATERSON & Co., Printers, 255, Ashton Old Road, Manchester, 11.

Wembley made a bold offer in an attempt to prise Frank Charles away from Manchester. Needless to say, EOS turned their offer down. Part way through the season, Belle Vue adopted the red race jacket bearing the black ace of clubs on a white triangle. Despite this, the name 'Aces' was still not referred to.

Belle Vue had a team mascot who travelled from London to Manchester whenever possible. Bob Staye, from Norbury, covered in excess of 7,000 miles during the course of the season to support his team. The club entered the sixth season of speedway full of confidence, but with the utmost respect for the other teams. Retaining the spoils of 1933 was to be a tough challenge and the resolve of the riders tested to the full. To give the riders a feel for racing, Belle Vue opened its doors on 31 March with the Silver Wheel Trophy. Two more meetings of this type took place, with the expected team taking on and beating 'The Visitors' 36-18 in a final warm-up.

Belle Vue's first opponents were Wimbledon, whom EOS saw as a real danger. Many times in the past the Dons had taken wins over Belle Vue. Confidence oozed as a good Wimbledon side was methodically taken to pieces. Knowledgeable authorities confessed at this early stage that they could not foresee any team matching the Manchester club's all-round power. As the season progressed, that prediction was not far from the truth. Their great rivals, Wembley, had different ideas and matched Belle Vue win for win for a great part of the season. At Wimbledon, the skipper Varey proved his value to the team. After two point-less rides, he unselfishly stood down from his remaining rides at a track he acknowledged he found difficult to ride.

If the team were ever to receive a wake up call, the visit of New Cross provided it. They came out fighting from the start and came close to embarrassing the champions. With seven races completed, the side was 2 points down and under severe pressure. It was Langton and Varey who threw the lifeline in the penultimate race, leaving the result resting on the last race. Tom Farndon won the heat, but Kitchen took second place and with no other finishers, Belle Vue won by a point.

A trip to Lea Bridge followed and was a fruitful one, with the riders having an easy time; Varey and Grosskreutz had maximum points. The three wins placed Belle Vue in top spot, but questions still had to be answered. Wembley was due in Manchester for their first great clash of the season, and only after this would EOS be in a position to assess his team's chances. Past meetings between the giants had been highly charged affairs, so why should this year be any different? West Ham was the next to try their luck in Manchester, but this ended up as a damage limitation exercise.

Bob Harrison was the rider who was unable to command a place in the team proper, such was the quality of the others. With any other club, Bob would have been guaranteed a place. However, he was Belle Vue through and through; not once did he ever suggest moving on, preferring to fight for his place. Harrison rode at many other tracks in open events to keep his riding sharp.

Much hype was given to Belle Vue's 'rising to the occasion' for Wembley's visit and perhaps this spurred on the Lions. They tore into the home side and achieved what many deemed the impossible. Wembley's 28-26 win stunned their 35,000 partisan 'friends'; that is not to say the crowd did not afford the triumphant Lions generous acclaim. Even the most biased Manchester supporter appreciated a team prepared to come out fighting.

After this setback, the team went on a run of seven straight wins. The closest margin in these was at West Ham. Lea Bridge, Harringay and Wimbledon arrived with expectations high, but left deflated, with dented pride. This spell of good form during May left the club heading the table. Rivals Wembley were close by, but having ridden fewer matches; both teams had lost one match apiece. EOS realised that the motivation of the riders was the key factor; any slip would be pounced on.

Towards the end of May, the possibility of a Division Two forming became reality, but Belle Vue was not included initially. Originally, it was EOS who had submitted a plan for the formation of the lower grade to the SCB, which was accepted. Tom Bradbury-Pratt announced that it would be for London teams, plus Birmingham (a track he controlled). EOS was having none of this and put Pratt in the picture. Eventually, Belle Vue's application was accepted.

Two former Belle Vue trainees, Eric Worswick and Henry Walker, returned to the speedways. It was agreed that Walker could return to Belle Vue, but Worswick appeared with Birmingham. EOS also attempted to sign Larry Boulton (a member of the 1932 team), but he elected to stay with his job in London.

The month of May ended in an emphatic 33-21 win at Hall Green. Langton, Charles and Kitchen all recorded full maximums, a rare occurrence indeed away from home. Bill also managed to lower the track record in the last heat of the match.

Eric Langton had experienced a difficult time for several weeks. His form was below

Eric Langton greets former star Arthur Franklyn.

the standard he expected and caused concern in the Manchester camp. Langton, being the star he was, worked hard and his brother, Oliver, made sure the engines were running properly. After weeks in the doldrums, Eric suddenly burst back on the scene and looked more comfortable when Belle Vue visited Harringay.

June should have started with the match against Plymouth, but for reasons known only to them, the Devon side pulled out at the last minute. The match points were awarded to Belle Vue, as Plymouth forfeited the match. Hurriedly, arrangements were made for New Cross to come to Manchester for a challenge; the management appreciated New Cross coming at such short notice. The result came as a shock as the Londoners rocked the champions and won by 64-43. The event was full of incident. Heat four was a complete farce; Greatrex's motor blew up and Bill Kitchen fell avoiding a collision and was injured. Eventually, an attempt to re-run the race was thwarted when Ron Johnson was disqualified. The heat was cancelled with no rider left to participate. Worse was to come in heat nine, when Kitchen was a non-starter and Grosskreutz had engine failure. The visitors finished unopposed. Max and Bill failed to appear in their three remaining races, consequently gifting the Lambs walkover heat victories.

No sooner had Langton snapped out of his bad spell, than Varey's form declined, but his 'never-say-die' attitude was an inspiration to other team members. EOS took the opportunity to give his side practice on the Wembley track, by taking a team for a four-a-side challenge. Although the Wembley crowd gave them the 'bird', the exercise was a success with an easy win. Lions' fans eagerly anticipated the forthcoming league match with the northerners.

Belle Vue tasted a second league defeat, losing at New Cross by 10 points. Only Eric Langton warranted any credit, with the others looking strangely out of sorts. The team made amends when Birmingham visited. They struggled to keep pace with the home stars and remained rooted at the foot of the table.

A determined team lined up at Wembley on 14 June and returned victorious. The Lions were never allowed to mount a challenge in a match that many thought Belle Vue could not win. A thoroughly professional display, in which the visitors dictated the meeting, was crucial; now the sides had lost two matches apiece. Varey baited the Empire Stadium crowd by waving a flag with the words 'Come up and see us some time'. They were reluctant to boo as Frank was riding pillion with 'Ginger' Lees of Wembley.

Birmingham took on Belle Vue in the opening round of the National Trophy. The contest was quickly over for poor Birmingham, as they were crushed 81-27; the second leg becoming academic. At Hall Green, the home side could do little to cramp the style of the rampant Manchester side, who won by 69-36.

On the 23 June, the Division Two regulations were announced. Teams would be regulated by a grading system of 'A and B' class riders. In this directive, it was stated that a rider could not participate in Division One and Two matches on the same day. Further to this, each team would have five riders, one being the reserve. The intention was to run these matches prior to the main league match of the night. Riders would receive the following pay rates:

Riders guaranteed 30s (£1.50)
Riders finishing first 30s (£1.50)
Riders finishing second 20s (£1)
Riders finishing third 10s (50p)

A payment equal to first place would be paid to any rider finishing second behind his partner, over and above these pay rates. It is believed that this is the first instance of the 'bonus point' being awarded.

The Belle Vue reserve team, who took the nickname the Goats, had their first match on 30 June against Birmingham and won comfortably by 23-12. Sid Plevin, Jack Tye, Henry Walker and George Thompson made up the first side. During the course of the season, others were to ride on odd occasions. On the same evening, Plymouth finally made it to Belle Vue and they were demolished by 41-12, a result that consolidated their league position.

July was a vital month for Belle Vue; they remained unbeaten in the five official meetings. The expected difficult match with Wimbledon did not materialise, with the Dons losing heavily. Visits to New Cross, so often a graveyard for Belle Vue teams, had never been popular. No mistakes were made on this occasion, as the team delivered an important blow. The win moved the club further away from Wembley, who, by this time, had lost another match. A poor Birmingham team was swamped 40-12, as Belle Vue pressed on towards the league championship. The Dons returned to Manchester for the National Trophy semi-final and departed a battered outfit. Having been humbled at Belle Vue 80-27, Wimbledon's task was of monstrous proportions. The Plough Lane faithful watched in disbelief as their favourites were outsmarted. Over the two legs, Eric Langton was unbeaten by an opponent, as he led Belle Vue to the final. Great rivals Wembley awaited them for the third consecutive occasion.

The Goats met with mixed fortunes, as after four matches they sat mid-table, having won two at home and lost two away. Their problematic away form was to afflict them throughout the season as they encountered tracks strange to them. It was, however, an encouraging start. August began with bank holiday meetings with Birmingham and Harringay. Neither caused too much trouble, as Belle Vue was in superb form. West Ham surprisingly provided a close match and lost in a brave display 30-24, with the closest match for months. Wimbledon opened the door for Wembley, when Belle Vue went down by a single point there. At this time, Eric Langton embarked on a run of 36 consecutive wins, which included a dead heat with Varey. He scored $106\frac{1}{2}$ points out of a possible 108.

Wembley was one of the few teams that Belle Vue would want to visit Manchester on three Saturdays out of four. The 25 August clash whetted the fans' appetite – they always relished the Lions' visits. Belle Vue was not in the mood to allow Wembley any glory. The 35-19 win gave vital breathing space over their nearest rivals. On 1 September, the Lions returned for the first leg of the Trophy final. History repeated itself as Wembley was hammered 71-36 – definitely not the result their manager, Alec Jackson, had envisaged! He was left in even more shock as Wembley totally collapsed in their home leg. Belle Vue was an unstoppable machine and gave the Lions an embarrassing 74-34 thrashing. Grosskreutz and Langton were in supreme form and collected maximum scores at Wembley, so the National Trophy remained in Manchester. It was not as if EOS wanted to win in this fashion, he would have preferred a closer and more evenly contested final. A measure of Belle Vue's superiority was that Wembley did not win a single race on their home track – a phenomenal statistic!

The series of matches with Wembley was split by the visit to Harringay. The Tigers failed to beat Belle Vue and lost by 12 points. On 15 September, Belle Vue progressed to the semi-final of the ACU Cup after annihilating Wembley 79-29; surprisingly, this was achieved without the services of Eric Langton. Sid Plevin was drafted in at reserve, but was not called on to ride. Charles was unbeaten, while Grosskreutz would have been had his engine not played up. Another trip to Harringay was the reward and was scheduled for 29 September. EOS urged his riders to make a determined effort and secure another clean sweep of the domestic trophies.

He could not have been prepared for the 31-22 defeat the team suffered by bottom of the table Plymouth. Grosskreutz led the way with a maximum and smashed the track record, the others looked a pale shadow of their former selves and only Kitchen managed to win a race. Wembley was back in the race by a result that nobody could have predicted. In the away match at Walthamstow, Belle Vue put the Plymouth loss to the back of their minds and strolled to an easy 36-17 win. Two nights later in Manchester, Walthamstow lost 40-12 to a rampant Belle Vue side, who were now within touching distance of retaining the championship and, if they could win at Wembley, it would be an uphill struggle for the Lions to catch them.

Left: *Eric Langton.* Right: *Oliver Langton, 'Our Kid's' mechanic for many seasons.*

The Goats' season, after a reasonable start, deteriorated. A single win in their final eight meetings placed them next to the bottom of the Division Two table. EOS was already debating whether there would be a second team for 1935. Rumours were rife that the division would not operate the following year. Wembley battled manfully to keep in touch with Belle Vue and were confident that, once again, they could claw their way back into contention. EOS's boys had other ideas; they wanted things done and dusted as soon as possible. Clinically, Belle Vue subdued the home side by 31-23 and made it all but impossible for the Lions to surpass the 52 points they had amassed. Mathematically, Wembley *could* equal that total, but the point difference was very much in Belle Vue's favour.

A rainy evening at Green Lanes greeted the sides for the ACU Cup semi-final. This failed to dampen the spirits of either side. For most of the meeting there was very little between the teams and it was only in the last few races that Belle Vue gradually exerted their authority. The 62-45 success placed Belle Vue in the final to meet West Ham at Wimbledon, a neutral track. New Cross returned for Belle Vue's final home league match and, just as they had done in April, they provided perhaps the stiffest test of the season for the home team. Typically, it rained, but this did not prevent both teams excelling in the appalling conditions. Despite going down by 2 points, the Lambs' gallant effort was appreciated by the Manchester crowd. The win finally put the championship beyond Wembley. But having now achieved the main goal of the season, there was still the small matter of the ACU Cup final to settle.

The riders took their bow in Manchester on 13 October, as the fans bade farewell to their heroes. In a fitting finale to end a tremendous season's racing, Belle Vue took on The Rest in a challenge. But foremost in the riders' minds was the vital meeting on Monday. At Wimbledon, the final could have gone either way, as West Ham fought tenaciously. The result was in doubt until the end, but it was Belle Vue who triumphed eventually by 56-51. Having achieved unprecedented success nationally, EOS was left to ponder the future. He had moulded a fine side together, but would face the calls to destrengthen the Manchester side. He was, however, big enough to ignore the jealousy and planned a repeat of his team's successes that had been built on the basis of a solid team spirit and togetherness.

1935

Frank Varey had ridden in Australia during the winter season in a desperate effort to rediscover his form. Having previously announced his intention to retire, Frank returned, disillusioned, and stuck by his decision. Frank Charles added further woe to EOS's pre-season team building by retiring again; his father, who managed Frank's affairs, had died during the winter. Acquisitions to the line-up for 1935 were Eric Blain, Tommy Allott, William Birtwell and the out-of-retirement 'Acorn' Dobson, who were hardly replacements for Varey and Charles. EOS had persuaded the board to sanction the transfer and signing of Blain, itself a rare occurrence at Belle Vue.

The National League too had a different look. Hackney Wick replaced Walthamstow, but Birmingham and Plymouth had dropped out after difficulties in 1934. The numerical situation of the league dictated that only twenty-four league matches could be ridden; in addition, there would be the National Trophy and ACU Cup.

Harringay opened the Belle Vue season on a foul night; rain poured throughout the evening. Over 22,000 hardy souls braved conditions to see the Aces overcome the elements with a 45-26 win. In the first race, Langton's engine blew up, but encouraging debuts for Blain and Allott pleased EOS. Abbott was not fully fit and ought not to have

ridden. On Easter Monday, Tiger Stevenson, of West Ham, brought the Easter weekend to a close when he won the Manchester Cup in front of 28,000 supporters, the biggest Easter Monday crowd recorded at Belle Vue.

There was some experimentation with midget cars during the season. They had been given trials in 1934, but had not been successful. Problems had been noted with the cars, but these were rectified by technical alterations. Arrangements were made for the cars to make their debut on 6 May, Jubilee Day. They made regular appearances during the season.

When New Cross came for league duty, the appearance of Tom Farndon provided a bumper crowd. A comfortable 41-30 victory over the team considered to be their main rival raised hopes that the club was capable of retaining the

Frank Charles, who transferred to Wembley in 1935.

championship. At Wimbledon, Belle Vue sneaked a 37-34 win over a resolute Dons side. However, one remarkable incident showed the camaraderie that existed between the riders. Abbott took a customary heavy fall, after contact with Syd Jackson's machine. The race continued for two laps before Jackson, well ahead in the race, sportingly stopped and attended to Joe. An unconscious Abbott came round and, for unknown reasons, thought the team was going to lose. He insisted on taking part in heat eleven and actually led for two laps before dizziness forced him to slow down. His partner, Kitchen, had by now taken the lead, but Joe gained a vital point for the cause, and kept Belle Vue in first place.

Over the Jubilee weekend, two meetings were staged at Hyde Road. The most intriguing was the crucial clash with West Ham. Hoskins, as usual, complained bitterly about the lack of riders coming his way. And yes, the Belle Vue team was weaker than in previous seasons. The resulting draw between the two was one of the best seen at Belle Vue and managed to keep the crowd on their toes. A promise by EOS of a champagne supper when the Hammers won in Manchester, prompted Hoskins to arrange a challenge match. Needless to say, they lost.

Having retired during the close season, Frank Charles now showed his willingness to race again. Belle Vue could have gained by using his services, but Wembley had an injury crisis and turned to Manchester for assistance. In a hasty deal, Charles was lent to Wembley. Bitterness over the deal surfaced when Hackney, who had a weak side, felt that Charles should have been offered to them.

Left: *Tommy Allott.* Right: *Pete Jackson, track maintenance man.*

Bill Kitchen captured the Jubilee Cup at the Bank Holiday Monday meeting. During this meeting, Eric Blain's engine exploded and a piece of the cylinder wall hit a pillar in the stand. Frank Varey did appear at the Monday meeting, but only to drive a midget car, his retirement still intact.

May continued to be a productive month as Wembley received a sound beating at Belle Vue. Successes away from Manchester continued with good wins at New Cross and then Harringay. Wimbledon, another team feared by the club, provided no more than a nuisance value. This would have irritated one female Dons supporter, who called herself MEL. A constant barrage of letters to the *Belle Vue Bulletin* with her anti-Manchester rhetoric left many supporters simmering, but did generate a lot of talk on the terraces. May ended with the first defeat of the season, which was at Wembley, so often a stumbling block in the past.

Some had the opinion that the rot was about to set in after the Wembley defeat. EOS took great delight in taking his team to West Ham and coming away with the points. As he put it, 'There is life in the old dog yet', a warning he advised other teams to heed. Arthur Warwick took a nasty spill when the starting tape stuck underneath his mudguard and he was pitched from his machine; luckily no other riders were hurt.

In the opening ACU Cup meeting, Wembley felt the might of the team, when losing by 74-34 in Manchester. This was followed by a loss in London to Wimbledon. Eric Langton tried his persuasive powers on Oliver in an attempt to get him to ride again. Alas, Oliver was quite content to look after 'our kid's motors'.

Hackney Wick, despite not being a strong team, had given problems to a few opponents. Belle Vue discovered this as they took a narrow victory 37-35. EOS saw this as the most important of wins. He felt that Hackney would influence the outcome of the championship. Their chances were enhanced by two vital home wins over Wimbledon and then Wembley. They now held an 11-point advantage over New Cross. Another trip to Hackney nearly provided the shock of the season when the Wolves earned a draw with a gutsy comeback. Belle Vue were in a good position, with a 5 point lead and one race to go. Hackney gained the 5 points required to snatch a league point. Both visiting riders failed to beat the time limit. Belle Vue progressed to the final of the ACU Cup, where they would meet Harringay after wins over Wimbledon and Wembley. Tom Bradbury-Pratt put his foot in it by declaring that Harringay would win the final whoever they met.

Tom Stenner, a journalist, described the National Trophy first leg match at New Cross as 'the best since the sport began'. A record attendance saw the rivals tie at 54-54, setting up a mouth-watering return leg; this too was an epic. Belle Vue was pushed all the way and managed to finally win by 55-52. A semi-final contest with West Ham was their reward.

As July drew to a close, the visit of Hackney Wick posed little threat, but the trip to West Ham was a disaster for Belle Vue, who lost 39-33. Rumours that Varey wanted to race again gained momentum and the prodigal son returned in the home leg of the challenge match with New Cross. Unfortunately, Frank took more falls than points, but he was back with the only club he wanted to ride for. Belle Vue won the challenge by an overall score of 112-103. Another former rider also returned, when Walter Hull trans-

Eric Langton with Harringay's Jack Parker.

ferred from Hackney Wick for a small fee.

Belle Vue wiped the smile off Hoskins' face in the trophy semi-final. At Custom House, the team gave an accomplished display, losing by the odd point. In the return, the 64-43 win did not reflect the quality of the racing, with the Hammers giving Belle Vue a thorough test. 'Acorn' Dobson, the side's prankster, took a dummy revolver into the pits and waited for the expected outburst from Hoskins. Finally, Johnnie could stand no more and cracked. Calmly, Dobson produced the gun and shot Johnnie 'dead' with a blank cartridge, much to EOS's amusement.

EOS declared that his team now had the chance to prove they were 'The Finest Team in the World'. The only team standing between them and the two cups was Harringay. In the league, 8 points separated them from New Cross, with eight matches remaining.

Max Grosskreutz was not to know that he would be the last challenger for the British Individual Match Race Championship. Tom Farndon, the holder, lost his life in a track accident not long after this final defence. Farndon was held in high esteem by all involved with speedway racing, with the management showing this in their tribute to him. The championship was never raced for again following Farndon's death, until after the war.

14 August	New Cross	Farndon beat Grosskreutz 2-0
17 August	Belle Vue	Grosskreutz beat Farndon 2-0
19 August	Hackney Wick	Farndon beat Grosskreutz 2-1

August was a good month for Belle Vue. Their nearest rivals, New Cross, could not defeat them. To stay in the running for the championship, winning at Belle Vue was essential. Then at Wembley, the Lions were brushed aside 42-30, as the side pushed ever closer to retaining the championship. On 24 August, the visit of Hackney Wick still went ahead, even though there were three Manchester riders in the Test match at Harringay. So the Wolves grabbed the chance to do what all teams dreamed of doing – leaving with the league points. Bill Kitchen did not help the effort by arriving late and missing his opening ride. Hackney stuck to their plan and it worked. An undefeated run going back to 5 May 1934 was broken.

The four legs of the National Trophy and ACU Cup were arranged over four consecutive weekends. Belle Vue hosted the first leg of the ACU Cup final on 31 August, in

Bill Kitchen, Bob Harrison and Joe Abbott relax as Harry Shepherd looks on.

which Harringay was annihilated by 73-34. The home side had things very much their own way. Kitchen and Grosskreutz were paired together and were virtually unbeatable. The fact that they had been through so many major events together fostered a terrific team spirit.

There was hardly time to prepare before the sides met again at Harringay, in the National Trophy, first leg. This was the final that Harringay really did want to win. Scores of Mancunians travelled at the cost of 10s (50p) return, for this match. Even the Harringay fans had to admit that Belle Vue was a team in superb form. There was a distinct lack of fight in the Tigers, who could only muster three race wins out of eighteen. The 63-45 cushion put the team in a tremendous position for both cups.

Belle Vue made the most of track advantage and the first leg lead to win the National Trophy for the third successive season. The Tigers rode far better than on their last visit, but had no answer to the all-round power of Belle Vue. Grosskreutz was continuing his wonderful form and he scored maximum points in the 63-43 win. Apart from the Parker brothers, who secured over half of Harringay's points, the Tigers toiled against an unrelenting tide. With the first of the three trophies now firmly locked away, EOS set his sights on the next obstacle.

In between the cup finals, Hackney arranged a challenge event, Champions *v*. The Rest, in which The Rest claimed victory by 37-35. A curious matter happened prior to the match, when Belle Vue was afforded a congratulatory dinner. Hackney entertained the Manchester club as 'Champions', with the SCB, press and other London tracks being represented. Yet they still had five matches remaining and it was possible for someone to overtake them.

The retention of the cups was completed on 21 September at Harringay. For the second successive year, the ACU Cup returned to Manchester. Harringay, to their credit, made Belle Vue battle all the way during the 54-54 draw. The Tigers nosed ahead by a couple of points at the halfway stage. It was Grosskreutz who again remained unbeaten by any opposing rider, and Abbott who brought Belle Vue back into the match. At the conclusion, Mrs E.O. Spence accepted the trophy from Professor A.M. Low on behalf of the club. The boys were presented with keepsake replicas.

September ended with an away win over New Cross, who were still in mourning over the tragic loss of Tom Farndon. Belle Vue, in the past and in the future, fully understood the effect that something like this could have on a club. The win was essential, but a hollow one.

On 5 October, a double helping of racing was offered when Harringay and West Ham visited on league duties. The league championship was now secure and both matches yielded easy wins for Belle Vue; Harringay by 44-25 and West Ham by 46-26. Still no 'Champagne Supper' for Johnnie's boys! Two days later, Wimbledon gave Belle Vue a testing time at Plough Lane, before losing by a single point.

As a final encore on 12 October, a match was advertised as The North (Belle Vue) *v*. Australia. The Aussie side was in effect a Test side. The match was close, but Belle Vue finally beat Australia by 39-33. After this match, the awarding of the National League Trophy and replicas was made to the club and riders. The actual trophy was presented outright to Belle Vue to mark the third consecutive year of winning it. The evening closed in spectacular fashion, with EOS arranging a coloured torchlight procession. The stadium was completely darkened to gain maximum effect, as riders, officials and track staff marched around the famous stadium. Despite the celebrations, the season was not yet over; Belle Vue had one last match at Harringay, which they lost.

The usual calls for Belle Vue to be weakened had already started. Would this mighty side be as effective in 1936? If EOS had anything to do with it, Belle Vue would be back as strong as ever and ready to fend off any challengers.

Eric Langton and Jack Parker shake hands before the 1935 National Trophy Final.

1936

The satisfaction of finally winning the championship in 1933 was a realisation of EOS's dreams. Defending it against mounting opposition and winning it three times consecutively represented a mammoth effort by the club. Belle Vue were to rely on the trusted riders who had steered them from one triumph to another. In addition to the 'big six', the team was comprised of Walter Hull, now back full time, 'Acorn' Dobson, Tommy Allott and Oliver Langton, who would ride whenever required.

Again the club had resisted the calls for the team to be weakened. Perhaps the monotony of the Manchester club claiming all the silverware did aggravate others. To do this, a team had to have consistency and Belle Vue had this in abundance. If anyone wanted to wrest the championship from them, they had to do it on the track and not in a backhanded way. An article written locally highlighted the arguments of their southern counterparts that they were tiring of the northern domination. EOS was not unduly bothered with the gathering anti-northern rift at London tracks. Even the increasing use of midget cars met with a lukewarm reception, as many thought EOS was trying to steal a march on them.

Bill Kitchen and his father became shareholders in the newly-opened Stanley Speedway at Liverpool. Other parties were involved in the venture, amongst them was Henry Skirrow, who raced midget cars. Oliver Hart Senior was the chairman and his sons, Stan and Oliver, rode for Liverpool.

During the season, some of the riders were used as part of a film named *The Cotton Queen*, which was a portrayal of Lancashire life and amusements. Filming started in the gardens and moved to the stadium for the evening meeting. Varey and 'Acorn' Dobson kept the cameraman busy, when displaying their skills, together with a 'few falls' to add to the excitement. Footage of the Third Test between England and Australia was also shot; the film was produced by the Rock Studios of Elstree.

The first traceable reference to Belle Vue being known as the Aces came in early April. Later, during the month of June, a supporter suggested that they should be nicknamed 'The Aces'. Her husband had himself referred to them as the Aces since 1930.

The season had opened on 11 April with a series of individual meetings to give the riders practice. West Ham was the first to face the Aces in league action and gained a surprise win, which started tongues wagging that, perhaps, this was the season when the Aces would be deposed. In a swift reply to the doubters during the second league match, Harringay toiled to stay in touch with the Aces. Grosskreutz was riding as well as he had ever done and bagged a maximum 12 points in the match.

More ammunition was given to the doubters when Hackney Wick demolished the Aces 44-21 at Hackney. In a sensational race four, there were no finishers. All four riders had fallen at some stage and, despite efforts to push their machines, all

of them exceeded the time limit. Eric Langton was absent, but this was no excuse for such a dull performance. EOS fumed at the display and it was his strong words of wisdom that finally kick-started the Aces into action. A run of five wins followed, which included victories at New Cross (where Langton again missed the meeting as it was 6 May, his unlucky day) and Wembley. By the middle of May, the Aces were sitting in their customary position at the top of the league.

Belle Vue's home match with Hackney Wick on 16 May was a sad one indeed. The Wolves had been dealt a blow on the previous evening, when star man, Herbert 'Dusty' Haigh, lost his life in a track crash. 'Dusty' was always a popular figure in the north and during his stay with Belle Vue in the early 1930s.

Eric Langton took part in a novelty race at Yeadon aerodrome, Leeds, on 6 June. As Langton raced on a set course, the aeroplane took the same route, but, as hard as Eric rode, he could not beat his winged rival. The event was staged in front of a sizeable crowd.

West Ham once again made it a bad start for Belle Vue in the ACU Cup, beating them 56-40. This loss was redressed when the Hammers had few answers to the

Belle Vue, 1936. From left to right: Bill Kitchen, Max Grosskreutz, Oliver Langton, 'Acorn' Dobson, Tommy Price, Joe Abbott, Bob Harrison, Frank Varey. Sitting: Eric Langton.

Arthur 'Bluey' Wilkinson.

Frank Varey returned full time in 1936.

might of the Aces. Joe Abbott was now back to his best and, together with Grosskreutz, formed a formidable spearhead. Not that there was any lack of track action. 'Bluey' Wilkinson, as usual, made life difficult and delighted the expectant crowd with his talents. Wilkinson returned a week later and won the World's Championship round with ease.

In the remaining matches, Harringay was beaten comfortably, both at home and away. However, poor Hackney, still reeling from the Haigh tragedy, were never in with a chance. At their home track, the 57-38 loss was a far cry from the Aces' last visit and at Hyde Road, the Wolves were dismissed 65-30 in front of a 30,000 crowd. The 326 race points amassed were more than enough to see the Aces through to the final, where they would meet Wembley in July.

Wimbledon had raced two further league matches and taken over the top spot from Belle Vue, who was now involved in further cup action. In the first round of the National Trophy, West Ham provided the opposition. The Aces' big fear was that they would once more stumble at the East London track, where they had never enjoyed great success. Fears were quickly dispelled, although the Hammers got off to a good start and led 9-3 after two races. From here on, Belle Vue gradually pulled away and led 31-23 at the halfway stage. Max Grosskreutz was magnificent; yet another maximum was gained with the minimum of effort. His partnership with Kitchen, who dropped 2 points, was nothing short of sensational. The final score of 65-43 left Belle Vue in a strong position. The tie was completed with a 68-40 (133-83 on aggregate) win, with Bill Kitchen unavailable. A semi-final beckoned with old adversaries, Wembley, which would take place after the ACU Cup Final against them.

League racing recommenced when Wembley arrived in Manchester, full of hope that the Aces could be beaten. Handicapped by the absence of Grosskreutz, who had a broken rib and neck strain, Belle Vue faced the prospect of a tough meeting. The poor form of Eric Langton did cause some concern, but it was Abbott and Kitchen who rescued the situation, as the Aces gained a 41-30 victory. They received solid backing from Bob Harrison, who responded in the Aces' hour of need. Sometimes, a team needs a lucky break and Belle Vue received theirs when Wembley lost the services of two riders. Gordon Byers and Frank Charles crashed and took no further part in the meeting. This left the Lions with one rider only in the last three races.

New Cross tried in vain to halt the Aces and gave a good account of themselves when losing 36-32. Max was still injured. They took a 3-0 first heat win when Nobby Key was the sole finisher. The tone of the match was set when neither team was able to forge a big enough lead. Belle Vue held a 3-point advantage going into the final heat. Requiring first and second places to record a shock win, New Cross saw their chance disappear when Jack Milne had engine failure.

Sandwiched in between the league matches was the Third Test, in which England defeated Australia by a massive 70-38. Belle Vue was well represented by Langton, Kitchen and Abbott, who all contributed double-figure scores. Hyde Road had the biggest crowd recorded at that time for any Belle Vue sporting event. Estimates put the attendance at 45,000 to 50,000. There were around 6,000 locked outside, after the police ordered the gates to be closed. The programmes sold out twenty minutes prior to the start of racing.

Success in London continued as Wimbledon lost by 38-30 and the Dons fared no better five days later in the return, losing 43-29. This meeting was run on a rainy evening, which affected the attendance. Those missing spectators were the losers, as the Dons rode with great heart and made the home side sit up. They were now firmly back on top of the table and covering well for the absent Grosskreutz.

Belle Vue now faced their first real challenge of the season in the ACU Cup Final. The first leg was ridden at the Empire Stadium. Wembley were expected to win and take a substantial lead for the second half of the final. Belle Vue had other ideas and came away with a loss by the closest margin possible, 48-47. After being inconsistent for many weeks, Eric Langton found his form and remained unbeaten. Throughout the meeting, there were never more than 3 points separating the teams, as the lead swung one way and then the other. Spectators must have been confused to find Tommy Price riding for the Aces and the Lions. Belle Vue had signed Tommy Price, the captain and a director of Liverpool, especially for the ACU Cup Final to make up the team numbers; he was, however, to continue riding with Liverpool. Wembley's Price was not related to the Aces' rider.

Two nights later, Belle Vue made it three final wins in a row, in front of 30,000 spectators. The result was in doubt until the closing races. After fourteen hard fought heats, the scores were tied. With the crowd at fever pitch, Varey and Abbott sped away from the start and secured a 4-point advantage with a race to go. Kitchen made no mistakes and ensured that the trophy remained in Manchester. Encouragingly for Belle Vue, the win had been achieved without the services of Grosskreutz. It would not be long before the sides were to meet again in the National Trophy semi-final.

League matters were resumed

Stanley 'Acorn' Dobson.

at Hackney, where the Aces had a 39-32 victory that strengthened their championship hopes. The following evening, it was the semi-final with Wembley, who must have wondered what had hit them. All seemed well after two races, with the Lions 2 points to the good. Grosskreutz, now back from injury, and his partner, Kitchen, restored the lead to the Aces. From that point, the Lions were totally outclassed and on the wrong end of twelve 5-1 heat results. Langton led by example, with an impeccable show of riding, as did Kitchen. Both riders had maximum returns.

Before the return leg with Wembley, the Aces visited West Ham for a vital match and made no mistake when recording a 44-27 win. Once again, Eric Langton proved there were few better riders than himself when in good form. Even 'Bluey' Wilkinson had to give second best to Eric, a rare feat at West Ham.

Wembley fought like 'Lions', although their task was a difficult one. Their 54-53 win over the Aces was a thriller all the way. Led by Lionel Van Praag, Wembley at one stage held an 8-point lead, before Belle Vue reduced the deficit with some steady riding. Grosskreutz maintained his comeback form with 14 points and helped the Aces to a fourth consecutive final.

Harringay became Belle Vue's opponents over the bank holiday weekend. On the Saturday, the Aces came away from Green Lanes with an 8-point win and followed this up by putting the Tigers to the sword, winning by 50-22. At the fourteenth attempt, Belle Vue's run of wins came to an end at Wembley. The Aces lost by 3 points and this was achieved without the services of Varey (dropped from the side), Harrison and Abbott (both injured). Belle Vue's Tommy Price made another Wembley appearance, but could only muster a single point as Wembley took advantage. By winning, the Lions had closed the gap on Belle Vue, who held a 10-point lead but had ridden four more matches.

In the World's Championship rounds, Eric Langton headed the qualifiers for the final. The resurgence of form had come at the correct time for Eric and he took 13 bonus points forward to the event. At the Belle Vue round on 8 August, Langton scorched to a maximum and made himself one of the fancied runners.

The Aces swiftly took revenge on Wembley, winning by 45-27 in convincing style. The threat of rain held off long enough to run most of the league match before the heavens opened and reduced the racing to farcical proportions. Racing was abandoned after the main event as conditions deteriorated quickly.

One week prior to the Trophy Final with Hackney Wick, Tommy Allott was freed by the club and signed up by Hackney Wick, a shrewd move! A big crowd assembled at Hackney to watch the first leg and it was the Wolves who triumphed, to the delight of all non-Aces' followers. As far as the Aces were concerned, the chief culprit for the loss was Eric Langton, who managed 3 points and was replaced by his brother in later races. Grosskreutz was the saviour with another full score, and but for his contribution the Wolves' lead would have been greater.

Once again, there were cries for Belle Vue to have riders taken away, to stop their continual winning of everything. Yet, in fact, the Aces were no stronger in reality than some of the other teams. Their reserve cover was poor and they already had Abbott missing for the rest of the season with a broken arm. Another injury would

Franklyn and Varey meet before the 1936 National Trophy Final at Belle Vue.

have been catastrophic to the team. Perhaps the biggest plus for Belle Vue was the team spirit. The defeat at Hackney proved that, with the correct application, the Aces could be beaten.

Anticipating a good meeting, 40,000 spectators packed into the Hyde Road stadium for the second leg of the trophy final. Grosskreutz was now showing his best form ever, with another faultless display. The tragedy was that he was not in the World's Final, having been injured during the qualifying stages. A victory of 73-31 made it four National Trophy wins in a row – a magnificent achievement. Varey had a lucky escape when he overslid and was narrowly missed by the oncoming riders. Only the league championship now stood between Aces and another clean sweep of all domestic trophies for the fourth year on the trot.

The wheels came off at New Cross, where Belle Vue put on a dismal performance, losing by 43-27. Only Langton rode with any conviction; the rest had an off night. Wins at home to Hackney Wick and away at Wimbledon, moved the Aces within one match of retaining the title. EOS was not a happy man after the 42-30 loss at Harringay – still short of that elusive win! Subsequent losses by Wembley kept the championship in Manchester by a 7-point margin.

Eric Langton came so close to becoming the first official World Champion at Wembley on 10 September, after a dramatic run-off. It later transpired that an agreement had been made. Allegedly, their pact was that the rider who was leading into the first bend, was to be the champion. This fact became common knowledge in Manchester after the final. Eric made the start, but was passed by Van Praag. Langton, bitterly disappointed at the outcome, took the result with dignity.

West Ham, who was at the foot of the league, came to Manchester and nearly sprung the shock of the season by holding Belle Vue to a draw. The Hammers became the only team to come away from Manchester with a league point in 1936. Wilkinson led the Hammers, with Atkinson giving stout support. The riding of young Ken Brett raised a few eyebrows and he gave a good account of himself. West Ham drew level in the ninth race and it stayed that way to the end. A pulsating final race, in which Kitchen was pushed hard by Wilkinson on the final turn, had the crowd spellbound. Wilkinson failed by inches to win the point that would have given the Hammers a deserved victory.

As the league programme drew to a close, the Aces, champions again, defeated a Wimbledon team that showed little stomach for battle by 55-17. Belle Vue's season ended with a series of challenges against teams wanting to topple the undisputed 'Finest Team in the World'. The Champions *v.* The Rest challenge was held at Wimbledon, where the Aces won by 40-31. Belle Vue, inspired by Kitchen's maximum return, cruised to a 43-29 win in a dull meeting at Hyde Road. Grosskreutz took three unbeaten rides before standing down in favour of Oliver Langton.

The final act of 1936 was a farewell meeting on 17 October, followed by a torch-light parade (a repeat of 1935). By way of saying thank you, the Belle Vue management dedicated the meeting to the riders, who had served them loyally for the last four seasons. The proceeds from the meeting were donated to the team, as recognition of the club's appreciation for their efforts. At the time, it was thought to be the first occasion that the proceeds of a meeting were to benefit a team.

After four years of unsurpassed successes, many could see that the following year was not to be an easy one. Abbott was still suffering with his badly broken arm. EOS realised that it was reserve cover that was lacking. If a realistic challenge was to be mounted, this situation would have to be addressed.

Jackie Hargreaves.

Belle Vue, 'The Finest Team in the World'.

1937

Although it was not apparent at the time, the Belle Vue bubble was about to be deflated. Gone from the 'Invincible Team' was Max Grosskreutz, now retired and looking forward to opening a speedway of his own at The Firs Stadium, Norwich. Belle Vue's loss was Norwich's gain. In 1936, Max was the outstanding rider at Hyde Road and replacing him was impossible. Although still an attractive side, Belle Vue recognised that there would no longer be any easy meetings. Other teams had strengthened up and wanted to topple the Manchester club from their lofty perch. Chun Moore came out of retirement to give cover, but failed to find his past form and transferred to Norwich later on.

Retirement and Joe Abbott were, it seemed, inseparable. The question of 'Will he, won't he?' thankfully was answered when the 'Iron Man' signed his 1937 contract. His only problem was the arm he broke late in the 1936 season. The bone had not knitted together properly and had been medically broken twice before any progress was made. However, EOS was adamant that no foreign rider would be recruited at Belle Vue; he preferred to bring along English juniors. During the winter schools, he had found two prospects. Jack Gorst, who hailed from Liverpool, and Len Eyre, whose son, Ken, rode for the Aces from 1968 until 1972, both possessed the qualities EOS demanded. It later transpired that he had shown a tentative interest in Wilbur Lamoreaux, who eventually went to Wimbledon. Lammy was close to becoming an Aces' rider, but circumstances dictated that he signed for the Dons.

A new training track at Hazel Grove, Stockport, was to be opened. Initially, the surface would be grass, but, when the funds became available, cinders would be used. The Manchester Motor Sports Club was to oversee the running of this new venture. EOS, too, would be keeping an eye on the progress of the riders.

The death of Clem Beckett in Spain saddened the Manchester public and many others. Beckett was one of the

1937 programme cover.

early sensations in the north and his duels with Varey and Franklyn would forever live in the memories of those lucky enough to have seen him ride.

A side composed of London riders arrived to open the Belle Vue season. George Newton gave the excited crowd a dazzling display of racing. It did not take Hoskins long to raise the blood pressure of Manchester folk, by describing the Aces team as a 'tribe of New Guinea head hunters'.

Vile conditions prevailed for the opening home league meeting. Hackney Wick and the Aces endured a mud bath to give some exciting races. The 47-37 victory flattered Belle Vue, for whom Harrison and Kitchen remained unbeaten. However, the quality entertainment given was a credit to both sides. Abbott was soon in trouble. In the warm-up match with New Cross, Joe was injured once more, although thankfully his arm was not damaged. Another fly in the ointment was Frank Varey proposing to ride in home matches only. The garage business at Riddlesden was taking a heavy toll on Frank. EOS gave his star a pep talk and soon had him back as a full time rider.

The real test for the club's ambitions lay in the opening matches against quality opposition. Away at New Cross, a tentative performance allowed the home team to win by 51-33. Hearts missed a beat when first Kitchen, and then Abbott, had nasty falls, but with no ill effects. Hoskins revelled at the 45-39 victory his West Ham team claimed, ending a proud record that went back to 24 August 1935 when Hackney Wick was the last side to win a league match at Belle Vue.

The consistency needed was not there; Abbott tried his best, but held back from riding in his normal reckless style. In his mind, he felt that his arm needed more time to regain full movement. Added to the lack of form shown by Eric Langton, it was easy to see why the Aces struggled away from home. Langton had other matters on his mind. He had recently become a father and asked his great friend, Max Grosskreutz, to be the godfather of the little boy, who was christened Max Anderson Langton.

Any match with Wembley was special and more so the clash on 1 May. If the Aces

Walter Hull returned to Manchester in 1937.

were to get their campaign back on track, what better way to do so than by beating the Lions 48-36. A fighting display helped to erase the shock defeat by West Ham the previous week and gave confidence for the away match at West Ham. Again the Hoskin's magic continued as the Hammers held Belle Vue comfortably and retained the premier spot in the division. A poor Wimbledon team was thrashed 62-22 at Hyde Road, a scoreline that astounded everyone; it was Wimbledon's fifth defeat in a row. The Dons' cause was hindered further by the unexplained non-arrival of Syd Jackson.

For the Coronation Gold Cup, Belle Vue entered two pairings, firstly Langton and Kitchen. Although they looked solid, they lost by 1 point. West Ham's 'Bluey' Wilkinson and Arthur Atkinson won the cup and Langton and Kitchen were runners-up. The other Aces pair, Abbott and Harrison, finished in third spot.

Harringay boss, Tom Bradbury-Pratt, had a dig at the Aces' problems, pouring scorn on them. Pratt indicated that it was not before time that, 'the once mighty Aces' should have a dose of their own medicine. He had picked an inappropriate time to make his comments, as Harringay was due to visit on 17 May. Belle Vue won by 52-31, a score that flattered the Tigers. Injury to Oliver Langton, who broke a wrist trying to avoid a collision with 'Tiger' Stevenson, deprived the Aces of his services. The promising youngster, Len Eyre, was given a chance at reserve and managed to score his first league point, despite his handlebars snapping in two. Len had been 'knocking at the door' and was unbeatable at junior level.

The starting area was giving concern to some riders and quite a few had fallen, after finding it too grippy. EOS rightly pointed out that every track was bound to be different and that Belle Vue happened to have good traction at the start. The team was more than happy with this, as the racing was much tougher for them this year. Hard racing was not the case in the challenge with New Cross. The young star George Newton had broken his leg and missed the match, much to the disappointment of the crowd.

Joe Abbott, now more or less back to his true form, won the International Trophy in the company of riders that would have graced a World Final. It was a pity his team-mates did not show Joe's spirit at Hackney Wick, when losing another match that they ought to have won. At Wembley, it appeared that the Aces were, at last, set to win an away match. Cruelly, the match slipped away when Abbott had a recurrence of an old injury; Wembley grabbed the chance and squeezed home 43-40. This left the Aces in mid-table with 8 points and with the look of an out-of-sorts team.

When the National Trophy rounds came about, most people's thoughts turned to Belle Vue. For four seasons, the Aces had dominated this competition and were determined to keep this piece of silverware. Wimbledon was the first obstacle to overcome; even they were shell-shocked after the 69-39 mauling at Plough Lane. And it was even worse for them in Manchester, as they went down 80-28, prompting their promoter, Ronnie Greene, to take the loudspeaker and apologise for his team's poor show. The fans and EOS were sympathetic and Greene's honesty was appreciated and applauded. EOS was rocked after the meeting when a newspaperman told him that Abbott's appetite for the sport had gone and that he intended to retire. Joe went on holiday, but came back to watch the Aces' match with New Cross on 19 June. EOS had other ideas and, after a few words of wisdom, Joe swapped his suit for riding leathers, but could only manage 3 points. Despite the win by 54-29, the Aces occupied fifth place, with EOS demanding more effort.

Rumours began to circulate that Belle Vue was to have an involvement at Liverpool. True, EOS was there, but only in an advisory capacity; he had taken Varey and Kitchen with him in an effort to boost attendance figures. Speculation rose again when Liverpool received an ultimatum to race on a Wednesday or not at all.

Visits to Harringay and Wimbledon yielded much needed away successes. The wins coincided with Oliver Langton making his return after several weeks out with a broken wrist. As a result, the Aces rose to third place, just 4 points adrift of West Ham, but could the run be sustained? More importantly, EOS thought it could.

The annual test matches with Australia had been abandoned and replaced with a series against an Overseas Team. In the Belle Vue test, Joe Abbott rode like a man possessed, scoring 15 points for England. Throughout the match, no more than 6 points separated the sides. With a race remaining, England held a slender 2-point advantage. Cordy Milne led to the first bend and fended off Abbott's challenges. Lionel Van Praag managed a third place to square the match at 54-54.

At last, the worst kept secret in the north was revealed when Belle Vue took over the running of the Liverpool team, who became known as the Belle Vue Merseysiders. EOS had negotiated a deal with Liverpool for the good of speedway racing. He was fearful that the Provincials could disappear, but at the same time, it would provide a training ground for aspiring youngsters. The first match was to have been on 15 July, but this was put back by a week, when Norwich, managed by ex-Ace, Max Grosskreutz, would visit.

Belle Vue Merseysiders, 1937. From left to right, standing: Tommy Price, Len Eyre, Stan Hart, Oliver Hart, Ernie Price. On bikes: Charlie Oates, Eric Blain, Alan Butler.

Walter 'Chun' Moore.

The next three matches would make or break the Aces' season. As holders of the National Trophy and the ACU Cup, it was vital that the club at least held on to one of these. Hackney Wick stood between Belle Vue and a sixth consecutive trophy final. In the ACU Cup, West Ham and Hackney Wick were in the Aces' group. An injury to Bill Kitchen could not have come at a worse time. This happened when Bill's boot was torn open and he suffered a burst vein. The accident prevented him from riding in these matches.

Not for the first time, West Ham dented the Aces' pride, by inflicting a 10-point defeat. Perhaps it was not too bad as Belle Vue had Kitchen and Hull absent, with Hargreaves and Dobson as replacements. In the National Trophy at Hackney, the Aces fared far better than usual, as they refused to let the Wolves build a substantial lead. Varey gave his team-mates a scare when he fell in the opening race and dislocated a shoulder. He had it put back immediately and was an inspiration to the team, scoring 11 painful points. Entering the last race on level scores, the Wolves took a maximum heat score to win by 4 points. Abbott had fallen in that race and was not able to contest the rerun. Any hopes that the Wolves would spring a surprise result at Belle Vue had evaporated by the halfway stage. Dicky Case was the only visitor to mount a serious threat; his comrades had a bad night. The aggregate win, by 121-95, put the Aces in the final, where they would face New Cross.

A small, but enthusiastic, crowd welcomed the Merseysiders to Belle Vue and they were treated to a terrific night's racing. Norwich played their part, but had to settle for second best in the end. The 59-46 win was an encouraging start and Southampton was given similar treatment one week later. Ernie Price looked a star in the making, with Stan Hart improving all the time. A team of English Provincial Riders rode against an Australian side, which included Bluey Wilkinson, in a Test match at Belle Vue. Price, Hart and Eric Blain represented the Provincials in the 60-48 beating by Australia.

Further defeats in the ACU Cup at Hackney and then at home to West Ham, gave the Aces an uneasy feeling. With a home match against Hackney remaining, Belle Vue had

Frank Varey on the injured list, pictured with a Belle Vue wrestler.

to win and win well. August started with two thumping home wins over Harringay and Wimbledon and a much healthier second place in the league. In the final ACU Cup match, Belle Vue had to win by 22 points or more in order to qualify for the final. EOS had the Aces in a fighting mood, plus the bonus of having Kitchen riding again, making Hackney's task impossible. The 69-27 trouncing saw the Aces in the final with their opponents being Wembley.

The first leg of the National Trophy final was held at Hyde Road, where the Aces amassed a 32-point lead to take to New Cross. EOS had altered his riding order to maximise the team's potential. For the final, he preferred to have Langton with Harrison and Varey with Abbott. The 40,000 excited supporters, who crammed the stands and terraces, roared the Aces on, hoping that they could hang on to at least one of their trophies. The old fighting spirit was still apparent, with crucial returns from Varey and Kitchen swinging the tie the Aces' way; only Jack Milne offered any opposition.

Belle Vue raised an objection over the use of Clem Mitchell by New Cross, as he had ridden in a previous round for Harringay. EOS had wanted to use Jack Hargreaves, but was refused permission because he had ridden for Liverpool in the early rounds. EOS, unhappy with the situation, viewed this as a way of trying to stop the Aces having further success. He need not have worried, for although New Cross gallantly pulled back some of the deficit, the task was too great. For the fifth consecutive year, the trophy came back to Belle Vue, the aggregate score being 115-100 to the Aces. The win was achieved at a cost; Bob Harrison fell and broke a leg, ending his season early.

On the same evening, the Merseysiders were riding at Hall Green, Birmingham, and were beaten by 53-31. However, it was the fatality to Stan Hart at the meeting that muted the Aces' celebrations. The accident happened during the tenth race. Hart was under no pressure, but fell heavily and was hit by another rider. Immediately, the race was halted to allow the stricken rider medical attention. The match was completed with the Merseysiders naturally showing little interest. During the second half, it was announced that Stan had passed away; after observing a silence, the racing was abandoned.

It was decided to go ahead with the meeting with Norwich on the following night and it was a subdued team that was heavily beaten 54-30 at home. From here on, their season deteriorated, with only two wins, against Nottingham and Norwich, in the remaining six matches. A final league position of fourth was an improvement. The team was in last place when they transferred from Liverpool. Attendance at these meetings appalled the management, considering the standard of racing, and was to have a bearing on there being no second team home matches in 1938.

From being a team challenging for three domestic trophies, the Aces' season fell apart. Everything that could go wrong did. In a run of nine matches, they could only muster three wins, effectively ending their grip on the National League Championship. Injuries now created the problem of not having any reserve cover. At Hackney, they lost out after being in a good position to win and then conceded second best to West Ham, who was striving for a first championship. In this meeting, Varey fell awkwardly, damaging his shoulder and took no further rides.

At this point, EOS gave the juniors a chance. For Hackney's visit, Price and Hargreaves were drafted into the first team. Price scored a creditable 3 points and Hargreaves only lost out to Cordy Milne and Dicky Case in his 6-point return. At New Cross, Wembley and West Ham, the scores ended as expected. Kitchen and Abbott kept the Aces in with a chance at New Cross, where World Champion, Jack Milne, reigned supreme. Bill did beat Milne, but the lack of back-up hindered the Aces. Wembley, by virtue of the win, held on to the slight chance of championship aspirations.

It seemed appropriate when West Ham finally clinched the crown against the deposed champions, with a 43-38 win. The Hammers were made to fight for the win and, with the scores level

Tommy Bateman.

113

Left: *Ernie Price.* Right: *Oliver Hart.*

and one race to go, the tension was felt by everyone, even Hoskins. Hargreaves and Hull gave their best, but to no avail as West Ham celebrated success. The friendly rapport between EOS and Hoskins was evident in the messages of mutual admiration that were exchanged. Both looked forward to 1938 when rivalries would start all over again.

With the championship finally gone, Belle Vue concentrated on the retention of the ACU Cup. A few days prior to the away leg, Wembley was beaten in the league at Hyde Road by 52-31, giving hope that winning the final was achievable and so it proved. Wembley only just scraped a 49-45 win as the Aces scored well throughout the team. The performances of Langton and Abbott tipped the balance and they received help from the others. Ernie Price was the surprise packet, with his 3 points scored. Two nights later, Belle Vue completed the task with a 61-35 win; again it was the high scoring of Langton, Varey, Abbott and Kitchen that steered the Aces home. With the contributions of the others, this was a supreme team effort.

On 16 October, the season ended with a double-header meeting. The Aces won their final league match against New Cross by 53-31 and the Merseysiders completed their league season with a 44-35 win over Norwich.

The season drew to a conclusion with mixed feelings. Fears that the loss of Grosskreutz would seriously affect the side proved to be well founded. This, together with the injuries at vital stages, finally toppled the Aces from their domination. However, the retention of the National Trophy and ACU Cup proved that the Aces were far from a spent force. The transfer of the Liverpool team in July had raised hopes that the lack of reserve power could be reversed.

In Ernie Price and Stan Hart, they seemed to have found two stars of the future; both were making rapid strides up the ladder. Sadly for Stan Hart, the glory was short lived as he paid the ultimate sacrifice at Birmingham; the prospect of a glittering career was suddenly gone. Ernie went on to hold a regular place in the first team during the latter stages of the season. He was instrumental in the cup fortunes of the club and EOS had high hopes that he would break into the team in 1938. He contemplated better times ahead, regaining the league championship his main goal.

1938

Belle Vue, having lost the National League Championship in 1937, was in a determined mood to regain possession of it. EOS was not one to sit back and allow a second season without the championship. He believed that, with the riders at his disposal, the championship could be reclaimed. It was not long before his plans took their first blow, when Joe Abbott crashed in Australia and broke his back. Although not necessarily out for the whole season, it was obvious that Joe would miss a big part of it.

Strong rumours circulated that the Norwich promoter, Max Grosskreutz, was to make a surprise comeback, but they were inaccurate. The good news was that Oliver Hart, a junior rider, had at last decided to continue with his speedway career. Oliver had not ridden since August 1937, when he saw his brother, Stan, killed at Hall Green, when riding for the Merseysiders. Oliver considered things and concluded that the best tribute he could pay to Stan was to continue riding.

In practice Frank Varey, at long last, looked at ease with himself. During the winter break, he had sold the garage business that had caused him so many problems and affected his speedway racing. The business had lost Varey a hefty sum of money and this had weighed heavily on his shoulders for two years. The main problem was customers not settling bills and he tended not to pursue these. On many occasions, Frank could be found working through the night on car repairs and then leaving straight from the garage to travel to London for a meeting. With the sale of the business concluded, EOS hoped that the real Frank Varey would again be seen.

The crowd attendance for the past three years had steadily risen; in 1937, Belle Vue surpassed the overall 1936 total by the end of September, with a month to go. It was hoped that this trend would carry the sport forward. Speedway attendance exceeded the Manchester City Football Club crowds at this time by a few thousand per meeting.

Gone were the days of 'Oh, Belle Vue will win', and West Ham boss, Johnnie Hoskins, sent EOS a pre-season message. He wished the 'Heathen' (Belle Vue) the best of luck, but stressed that his Hammers would again be champions. The progress of the Aces would be watched with sympathy and the wooden spoon sent to Manchester when appropriate.

Bill Kitchen, who had enjoyed a successful winter in Australia, returned home by boat. When the ship called at Marseilles, Kitchen disembarked and completed the journey home by aeroplane. From Le Bourget Airport, Bill flew to Croydon and then took the train. A taxi ride saw Bill in familiar surroundings at Belle Vue, where his bikes awaited him. The actual cost of the flight was £9 15s (£9.75). It was nearly a wasted journey. Belle Vue was due to open on 9 April, but a Rugby League Cup semi-final held in the afternoon left the track damaged, with litter covering the terraces. A despairing EOS had to hurriedly tidy up. However, the meeting went ahead, although a slick track was not to the riders' liking. The lack of loose dirt, caused by thousands of people on the track, was the main problem, but happily, there were no bumps.

An announcement was made that last season's second team was to continue, but not at Belle Vue. They were entered into the second division and the English Cup. In the end, the cup matches were raced at Sheffield, but no home could be found to allow the team to enter the league. On more than one occasion, they were referred to as the Colts, a name to be used again thirty years later.

Track accidents were to have a profound effect on the Aces for much of the season. In the past, injured riders had been covered by the reserves. At this time, EOS was finding it increasingly difficult to do this. Bob Harrison had recovered from his broken leg and was back in the saddle for the team selection match. West Ham and Wembley came for challenges, with only the Lions showing any fight.

A bad start in the first league match saw the Aces thrashed at New Cross 55-28. Feelings were stirred when a journalist suggested that more performances like this would make the Aces a second-half attraction. He was silenced when West Ham was beaten in the league at Belle Vue. To make matters worse, Joe Abbott was thinking of retiring again.

Away from Manchester, poor showings were the Aces' Achilles heel. Consistency had been a trademark for four fabulous seasons – this was but a distant memory now. Wimbledon walked over the Aces, but a 1-point home defeat of New Cross lifted spirits.

Back-to-back wins in matches with Bristol pushed Belle Vue up the table. Injuries had forced EOS to include Walter Hull and young Harold Jackson in the line-up at Bristol. Varey gave his orders that both riders were not to race each other and ensure that at least one of them finished, to guarantee an Aces' win. The following night, Belle Vue had an easier task against the Bulldogs, but at a cost. The injury bug struck again, this time with Eric Langton, whose bike landed on his leg when he reared at the gate.

Despite the loss of Langton, home wins over Wembley and Wimbledon kept the Aces in second place behind New Cross. Away from home, they could not break the losing sequence. Strength in depth was needed but was not there, and West Ham found them 'easy meat'.

Belle Vue hosted a Clubman's Speedway Championship, held behind closed doors, on behalf of the North-Western Centre of the ACU. One rider to show some promise was Ernie Appleby, who was to feature in the wartime meetings and just after the war, when he became involved with the Newton Heath training track. At the time, Appleby was a cotton mill worker and the earnings of a star speedway rider appealed to him. Henry Walker, who was discovered in 1933, began to practise again. Walker had been forced to give the sport up due to family problems.

Injuries affected both the first and second teams in June. Ex-rider, 'Chun' Moore, was asked to help out at Sheffield, when some of the reserves were being called into the main team for the trip to Wembley.

Frank Varey, who was acting as a steward at a grass-track meeting, became involved in a tragedy. He was asked to take a seriously injured rider to hospital with the doctor. Frank was driving carefully, when a child ran out and was struck by the car. Seeing that there was nobody around, they lifted the child into the car. Sadly, the child died before they reached the hospital.

Varey joined the injury list at Wembley and was hospitalised. He discharged himself and rode in the home match with Wembley. Not only was he unbeaten, he broke the track record and received £10 for this. Another home win over the improving

Wimbledon was tempered by a narrow defeat at West Ham. Surprisingly, the Aces maintained second place in the league.

Ticket sales for the First Test at Belle Vue were boosted by the inclusion of Max Grosskreutz in the Australian side. He had agreed to ride to assist the bid for the 'Ashes'. The 56-52 win by the 'Kangaroos' was not incident-free. Van Praag and Varey clashed, which saw Van Praag's machine riding the safety fence 'Wall of Death' style and the rider hurled up the track. How the bike did not go into the crowd, nobody will know!

Eric Langton had returned after his leg injury, but had not reached peak form. Now it was the turn of his brother, Oliver, to join the casualty list with an arm injury. Bill Pitcher had crashed into him, pinning him against the fence. Bob Harrison received boos from fickle fans after the Aces lost at home by 4 points to New Cross. Bob had blown his number one bike and his other was not quick enough. The match had been important to both sides. A win for the Aces would keep them in touch with New Cross – a loss made it all but impossible to catch them.

At Sheffield, the reserves were making steady progress in the English Cup. They reached the final by beating their hosts, Sheffield, at Owlerton, by 42-41. A two-legged final against Southampton, the Southern Section winners, would be run at the end of August. Wembley and Wimbledon ended the Aces' grip on the ACU Cup, which they had held since 1934. Home wins and away defeats against the same clubs signalled the end. Worse was to follow in the *Daily Mail* National Trophy, as Wembley ended the

Max Grosskreutz and Frank Varey prior to the Test Match.

George Cockbone – Belle Vue II.

Aces' four-year run by an aggregate of 2 points. The alarm bells were now sounding, both within the club and among the supporters. Now all that remained to fight for was the National League Championship and this was only the second week in July. Alarmists were making their feelings known, with the Aces in a situation they had never experienced before.

The reality of possibly not winning a trophy prompted critical letters to EOS about the team. Some said new riders were needed. 'No,' was his reply. He countered them by arguing that the racing was far closer than past seasons and crowds were still on the up. Therefore, he must be doing something right. A section of the crowd baited Cordy Milne of Bristol and Eric Chitty of West Ham whenever they visited. Fair-minded fans were angered by this and demanded action against this loutish behaviour. Chitty had clashed with Langton in 1937, but not to the extent that he needed to be treated badly.

After the defeat at Wimbledon, a group of Dons' fans tried to wind up EOS and received an unexpected reply. He congratulated them on their success, wishing them well for the future. EOS ended his reply with a dig at past comments, mentioning that he did not remember London clubs rushing forward to praise his team. The tone of his reply took the group by surprise.

The ACU Cup match with Wembley also saw the only 'home' appearance of the Sheffield based reserve side; they took on and beat a junior Lions' side. They had also visited Lonsdale Park, Workington and routed the home side.

Hopes that Joe Abbott would be fit enough to take his place in the World Championship Rounds ebbed away. He had raised the question of a return, but his doctor warned of the risks if he rode and took a bad fall. As a consequence, Abbott remained on the sidelines for the remainder of the season, not risking permanent disability.

Frank Varey was involved in a bizarre accident with Eric Chitty at West Ham. A piece of paper flew into the Canadian's goggles, temporarily blinding him and Chitty, unable to see Varey on his outside, crashed into him. Varey somersaulted three times before hitting the fence. Much to the delight of the crowd, Frank regained his senses and took his other rides. The match ended like many others, as Belle Vue lost emphatically 56-28.

The final league visit of the season of Wembley produced a close match and Belle Vue

Tommy Bateman – Belle Vue II.

was fortunate to escape with the 43-41 win. Next for the Aces was a visit to the unhappy hunting ground at New Cross. Another lacklustre display started a slide down the table. Varey was in the wars once more – this time picking up a chipped bone in his shin. Although his leg was in plaster, Varey phoned EOS and said he was riding in the Belle Vue World's Championship round. And ride he did, scoring 9 points! He followed this with a full score against Harringay on Bank Holiday Monday. Even EOS had to admit that Frank's performances astounded him. Praise indeed!

Varey chose to ride for the sake of the team, when he ought not. The club by now were resigned to Abbott missing the whole season and Eric Langton still looked a pale shadow of the past. An empty trophy cabinet now seemed inevitable and hurt the pride of the team as a whole. After all, success had been relatively easy for five years, so made it all the harder to accept.

No sooner had Oliver Langton returned from the injured list, than he was back on it. Riding in the Championship of the North event, Oliver had felt unwell prior to the start. After his race had ended, he passed out, while still seated on his bike. As he fell, the handlebar struck the back of his head. The crash added more chaos to the already depleted side and put more pressure on the top three to score heavily. The supporters had, at last, some good news when Varey, Langton and Kitchen qualified for the World's Final on 1 September.

Johnnie Hoskins brought his West Ham team north and humbled the Aces 47-36. Naturally, Hoskins was pleased to have put one over EOS's men. It was an embarrassing defeat – 'The Finest Team in the World' until recently! How EOS wished that the season had finished, even the trip to lowly Bristol yielded a blank return! The bottom of the table Bulldogs were despatched with little trouble the following night by 54-30.

A slide from second in the table continued, with the Aces still not able to win away. Luck was against them at Wimbledon, when Kitchen arrived late due to his train being delayed. Had Bill taken all four outings, the result would not have altered much. The home league programme ended on a high note, with the visit of the Dons, who lost by 50-34. This was an unsatisfactory end to a season that had started full of hope, yet

Left: *Fred Tuck – Belle Vue II*. Right: *Jack Gordon – Belle Vue II*.

ended in despair. In their last league match, the Aces succumbed to Harringay by 52-32 in a fashion that typified the season.

Just when everything that could go wrong, did, the reserves rescued the season with a surprise aggregate win over Southampton. The two-legged success produced the only silverware in the trophy cabinet. But it was Southampton who was the favourite to win. EOS travelled to Owlerton and must have been heartened by the fighting qualities of his young charges. They took the first leg by 47-36, with Hargreaves leading the way with 12 points. How Southampton made Belle Vue live on their nerves! A calamitous first race for the home team stretched the lead for 'The Colts' to 15. Southampton fought a gallant battle, but fell short of the required total by 3 points.

The season petered out with challenge matches against West Ham and Wembley. The farewell meeting was held on 15 October. By and large, the 1938 season had given little to enthuse about. The reserve side, however, had given hope that better times were just around the corner. Inadequate cover during the many periods of injuries had highlighted the lack of strength. When injuries did occur, they tended to be in twos or more, putting too much of a burden on inexperienced shoulders. If EOS had learned anything, it was that the Aces could bounce back if free from injuries. With a full strength team, they were equal to any other National League side.

1939

In 1938, the Aces' first team had only their second season without trophies, if you ignore the farcical 1929 league season, 1932 being the other one. EOS's great desire was to see his team topping the table again. To do this, a vast improvement was needed. Joe Abbott was now fit after missing all of the 1938 season. The 'Iron Man' had been sorely missed in 1938 and was crucial to helping in an upturn of form.

The previous season had thrown up an interesting statistic. Crowd levels were the best recorded in the ten years of speedway at Hyde Road despite the lack of success. EOS expected even higher crowds if the team could rediscover past fortunes.

For speedway, the situation in Europe cast a dark shadow, but for Belle Vue, the show had to go on. Seeing his team return to their former glories was EOS's dream and he may have achieved this had world events not taken over in September. The only 'war' he was interested in was against London.

EOS, as ever, was wary of the southern area promoters, as they had dominated the major events of 1938. Antagonism had existed between them and he really did not see eye to eye with Harringay or New Cross. He did have respect for Wembley and Wimbledon, as they went about their business with minimal fuss and bickering.

The key members of the Belle Vue team were Eric Langton, Frank Varey, Bob Harrison, Joe Abbott, Ernie Price, Oliver Langton, Jack Hargreaves and Bill Kitchen. Hyde Road opened the doors on 7 April with a challenge against arch rival Wembley to whet the appetite of the fans. The Lions were slaughtered 55-29 – Lionel Van Praag was unfairly booed by his own supporters; perhaps they did not realise that he was riding while injured. West Ham arrived the next night and did marginally better than the Lions.

The ACU Cup was renamed the British Speedway Cup and was raced for on a league basis. Wembley did not take part because they opened later than other tracks. The Hammers returned to Belle Vue a week later for British Speedway Cup duty and gave a subdued showing. Winning 59-36 gave the Aces a positive start to build on.

WEDNESDAY, JULY 12th, 1939.

VOL. 1. No. 1.
412TH MEETING.

BELLE VUE BULLETIN & PROGRAMME

PRICE 6D

Belle Vue, 1939. From left to right, standing: Ernie Price, Jackie Hargreaves, Joe Abbott, Bob Harrison, Bill Kitchen, Oliver Langton. On bike: Eric Langton, Frank Varey.

A Belle Vue second team visited National League Division Two side Stoke, in mid-April. At that time, the club did not run a reserve side. This trip offered a chance for the hopefuls to show whether they could cope with the rigours of racing at a higher level. Ironically, it was Stoke who folded a few months later and Belle Vue who took on their remaining fixtures. On a strange track the 45-38 loss was commendable and good experience.

Belle Vue and EOS in particular took the cautious approach in the early meetings of 1939. Quite a few Aces' riders had early season injuries, which gave concern to the management. Varey was riding with his leg in plaster – when was Frank not injured? Hargreaves had stitches in a leg wound that kept reopening with the pressure of the left leg on the track. Even worse were Eric Langton and Bob Harrison, who were riding with their legs in irons.

Although it did not prevent them from riding, the heavy programme of matches did not allow much time for recuperation. Even Walter Hull, now riding at Belle Vue again, suffered problems with lumbago. Overall, they were not a very healthy side, but with Abbott now coming back to something like his normal form and Bill Kitchen riding better than ever, things were not too bad.

EOS did have a mellow side to his personality. One particular bank holiday, a young boy cycled from Barnsley to Manchester to see the speedway. On arriving, he paid his entrance money and took his seat. At the time, Broughton Rangers, the Rugby League football team based at Belle Vue, were playing an afternoon match. He had come in thinking the speedway was on then. The match ended, the stadium emptied, but the young boy stayed in his seat awaiting the speedway match. A stadium groundsman noticed the lad sitting in the stands and enquired why he had not left the stadium. Even though he explained he had mistakenly come into the rugby match, the distraught lad was asked to leave and go to see EOS in his office. A clearly upset boy blurted out the sorry tale to the boss, who listened attentively. Realising he was telling the truth, EOS reached into his pocket and gave the delighted boy 1s (5p) for admission to the speedway and 6d (2½p) to spend on the amusement park rides and in the gardens.

The draw for the first round of the *Daily Mail* National Trophy was a good one, pairing the Aces with Wimbledon. EOS was happy with this, as his side had enjoyed much success over the South London side down the years.

Belle Vue had been experimenting with varying types of surface materials. One that showed some promise was the mixing of oil with the cinders. Tests were conducted with the mixture and it was found that the surface bound together far easier than normal. The track was more consistent, giving better tyre grip – the riders seemed quite happy with it. Safety was paramount to riders and they felt much more at home on the oily cinders.

New Cross came north at the end of April, but as a team was totally out of form. They stuttered to a 20-point defeat, which put the Aces in a healthy position. The run came to an end with a crash, literally. Although the Hammers avenged their loss at Belle Vue, Varey injured himself again. He took a heavy fall and was carried from the track. Worse was to come when he fell again in his next ride and was carried off once more. He withdrew from the remainder of the meeting.

Order was restored when Southampton was outclassed 63-33; the Saints were not a good side and struggled against most teams. Belle Vue's London bogey continued as they lost their third match on the trot at New Cross by 51-43. The visit to Banister Court, Southampton allowed the Aces to claw themselves back into contention. Although they were next to the bottom, only 5 points separated them from the top.

Early season pace-setters Harringay were put to the sword by a no-nonsense Aces' display. To win the cup was now a simple matter: Belle Vue had to win in London, at Harringay and then beat Wimbledon in the final match at Belle Vue. The Aces also had to score 100 points over the two matches. With the Aces engaged at Harringay, Belle Vue staged a Best Pairs event, at which Wembley's Lionel Van Praag shattered the track record, with a new time of 74 seconds on the reconditioned track. Part one of the equation was achieved, with a gritty performance at Harringay when it mattered most. The Aces won 51-45 – their only 1939 success to date in London and the first in the capital since 1937. The Dons made the journey north for the crunch match, which was played out in front of a partisan home crowd craving a win and they were not disappointed.

The Aces, spurred on by the lack of recent success, gradually built up an unassailable lead, eventually winning by 53-43. Jubilant scenes from the terraces and stands greeted the team – this was the first silverware won by the seniors since the National Trophy and ACU Cup wins of 1937. For EOS, sensing the good times returning, it was a sweet success. He was quoted as saying, 'London tracks are not bothered who wins, providing it's not Belle Vue.' He was critical of the speedway press due to the lack of coverage for Belle Vue.

At the end of May, Belle Vue had received a request from Southampton for Bill

Kitchen to be released on a transfer. Obviously, EOS listened, but issued a firm 'nothing doing' to Southampton. The Kitchen request was not the first that he had received. Moves had been made for several riders on Belle Vue's books, but, naturally, EOS opposed these too. Despite two season's decline in the team's fortunes, weakening the Aces even more was still a preoccupation of certain clubs. Eric Langton had tried several times to achieve the first 50mph lap at Belle Vue, which he considered a distinct possibility. Up to date, all attempts had failed and so did these.

The league programme opened with a close encounter with West Ham, with the campaign getting a winning start. Bill Kitchen was in trouble against Harringay, who gave the Aces another hard match. Bill was disqualified, after harshly being adjudged guilty of foul riding. Aces and Tigers fans agreed that it was an unfair decision. Nevertheless, the win kept a five-match winning streak intact. At Wembley, the Aces squandered the chance to put one over the Lions and lost by 16 points in a thoroughly miserable display.

Eric Langton leads Lamoreaux, Abbott and Duggan – Belle Vue v. Wimbledon, British Speedway Cup (3 June 1939).

125

Varey was often involved with anything mischievous and one instance was recalled many times. He and Eric Chitty decided to have a spot of fun with an air pistol, by shooting out windows in J and K stands at Belle Vue. EOS, unbeknown to them, had seen their game and waited for his chance. After the meeting, Chitty and Varey went to his office for payment. EOS handed Frank his pay packet with a deduction for the damaged windows. This was queried, but 'the gaffer' was adamant that Varey should make good the damage. Realising it was not a joke, Frank questioned him once more and received the same blunt answer. At this point, Frank pulled the pistol from his pocket and shot the lights out, leaving poor old EOS sitting in the dark! It is hard to imagine that happening nowadays!

With the 'clash of the titans' looming large, EOS wasted no time in publicising the fixture with Wembley. Before this, an away success at Southampton put the Aces in good heart for Wembley's visit. The Lions were boosted by the return of Frank Charles, back from retirement again. Lions newcomer Aub Lawson made everyone sit up and take notice with some spectacular displays.

The expected nail-biter did not materialise, as Wembley was no match against the Aces' powerful stars. The sensation of the show was Ernie Price, scoring 10 points, his best return to date. When the Aces rode at their best, it would have to be a good team to beat them. It appeared 'mandatory' that Abbott be carried off unconscious. His recent accident at Newcastle was followed by one in the Wembley match. He hit the fence at speed, but, thankfully, suffered nothing worse than concussion. Varey received a foot injury in his opening ride, and scored 8 points in his remaining races.

Price had, in fact, taken delivery of the Excelsior Speedway bike, originally pioneered by ex-Ace, Max Grosskreutz. He allowed Excelsior to produce the bike because of the demand. Bill Kitchen partnered Price and looked after him and, between them, they only dropped 2 points to the opposition.

Lions' boss, Alec Jackson, was full of praise for the Aces; he acknowledged that, on this form, Belle Vue could beat any team. The current champions, New Cross, were having a torrid time, languishing at the foot of the table. It would be the biggest surprise if the Aces or Wembley did not top the table, although Wimbledon had made up some ground.

Walter Hull re-appeared at a practice session in late June, with a view to making a comeback and he looked to have lost little of his racing expertise. Although he made no appearances with the main team, he did ride in many of the second-half events. Knowledgeable sources throughout Britain recognised Bill Kitchen as a favourite for the World Championship. Langton was still a class act, but Kitchen was now showing his true potential. Bob Harrison, who suffered a loss of form in early matches, was back to his best. Price, Hargreaves and Harrison were scrapping for a place in the team proper – a situation envied by many tracks.

Maintaining consistent displays held the key to success and the draw at New Cross, followed by a 63-21 trouncing of West Ham, consolidated the Aces' position. Yet again they were reminded that the road to success, sometimes, is a rocky one. Wimbledon boosted their chances without being troubled. A catalogue of motor mishaps hampered the Aces' progress. At this match, Ernie Price picked up a nasty injury – his

Stan Lemon – Belle Vue II.

foot became entangled in Wally Key's machine. Price's boot was ripped off, but he still continued in the meeting.

Once again, Belle Vue took on another team's fixtures, when, on 7 July, they were accepted into the National League Division Two. Stoke, having withdrawn from the league, transferred their team, with Belle Vue reserves also being added to the squad. Rather surprisingly, Oliver Hart was not included in the line-up – Belle Vue had loaned him to Stoke to strengthen them. Hart then tried his luck with Edinburgh, who had been refused membership of the league but was to ride in the Union Cup.

Stoke were at the foot of the table when they withdrew and, after the opening match with Sheffield, Belle Vue II were still rooted there. Consistency evaded the second team and the heavy loss was not surprising. Bill Kitchen warmed up for the big trophy clash with Wimbledon with an exquisite display in his quest for the World Championship and was unbeaten in his home round. The Dons stirred events up by describing the Aces as 'Heathens, who would be devoured Horns, Hoofs and All'.

EOS took it all in his stride and would allow his team to do the talking. Wimbledon must have wished nothing had been said as the determined Aces shocked the hosts to steal a 5-point lead. Varey, as usual, was in the thick of things and he nearly did not arrive at all. Frank waited for transportation to the track, but it failed to arrive. A team-mate eventually assisted him and it was his devilish on-track action that influenced the outcome.

One of the Aces' favourite sons departed this world on 15 July. Frank Charles, now at Wembley after coming out of retirement to assist the Lions, had in recent years developed an interest in gliding. He was killed when his glider came down at Great Hucklow, Derbyshire.

In Division Two, the leaders, Newcastle, struggled at Hyde Road and left with an unexpected 1-point defeat, to give the second team their first points. Norwich lost out to them as well; the aggregate score giving Belle Vue II a National Trophy semi-final place against Bristol.

Cup matches were never formalities. When Wimbledon returned for the second leg, only Wilbur Lamoreaux excelled. Without him, the Dons would have sunk without trace. Lammy would have remained unbeaten but for some gritty team riding from Varey and Kitchen. Written in a programme, the original owner has described this race as, 'One of the finest ever, on the great speedway'. Glowing praise of the titanic duel that Varey, Kitchen, Lamoreaux and Duggan gave before the massed crowd!

August started with the ARP (Air Raid Precautions) giving fire-fighting displays during the interval at Belle Vue – a sign of things to come. Belle Vue had five riders selected to ride in the Test match and also drew New Cross in the trophy semi-final.

Newcastle boss, Johnnie Hoskins, raised the roof with comments about the second team. He maintained the inclusion of Price and Hargreaves in the team, was unfair. Although they were riding in the first team, EOS only used them when needed. For the rest of the time, they had only raced second halves. The use of the pair had already been sanctioned and EOS viewed Johnnie's outburst as hot air. Tommy Bateman showed some excellent form at Newcastle and he gave George Pepper a run for his money – a rare feat at Brough Park!

Oliver Hart returned to Belle Vue for a Union Cup match with Edinburgh, who fully deserved a share of the match. An out-of-the-blue victory at Newcastle raised hopes that progress could be made in the competition. League form, however, remained indifferent. A win over Hackney Wick was scant reward for the effort given, yet in the matches at Bristol and Newcastle, both were lost. There were some strong teams in this section and no easy matches.

Australia came and failed to win the last pre-war test, when Langton, Kitchen, Varey, Abbott and Harrison were all chosen. Langton was 'dogged' by motor problems and Varey fell heavily, damaging his elbow. England won comfortably by 65-42, with Kitchen top-scoring with 16 points.

Although not apparent at the time, the visit of Harringay on 7 August was the last pre-war National League Division One match to take place at Hyde Road, with the Aces winning 54-30. All other matches after that were either cup or Division Two events. In the World Championship Rounds, Kitchen, Varey and Langton all qualified for Wembley. Kitchen was still pressing his claim to be champion, but riding equally well were Cordy Milne and Wilbur Lamoreaux, both worthy contenders. The club did organise trips to Wembley. This cost 16s 3d (81p) return by train from Manchester to Euston.

Belle Vue II came unstuck when Sheffield visited, losing by 6 points. In the return, Sheffield's impressive form

Ted Bravery – Belle Vue II.

Belle Vue's finest on Test duty – Joe Abbott, Eric Langton, Bill Kitchen, Frank Varey and Bob Harrison.

continued in an evenly contested match. Newcastle was beaten 52-32 in the last Union Cup match held. The matches against Glasgow were never raced.

In the National Trophy semi-final, the Aces went to New Cross, where they often had difficulty winning. To come away with a 64-44 win exceeded all expectations. Kitchen and Eric Langton were in supreme form, both netting 17 points apiece and unbeaten by any opposing rider. Undoubtedly, young Jack Hargreaves swayed the result, with 9 points. Although everyone contributed, Varey had an off night, giving an uncharacteristic display. From the start, the warning signs were there for New Cross as Aces' reserves, Price and Oliver Langton, surprised and outpaced the home pairing.

New Cross arrived for the second leg on 26 August with forlorn hopes and departed a battered side. The result was far worse than anyone could have foreseen, when Belle Vue recorded the season's best home victory, winning 80-28 (144-72 on aggregate). Even the reserves, Price and Hargreaves, each riding twice, took maximum points in their heats. By any standards, the South Londoners were outclassed. They could argue about Ray Duggan being injured, but it is doubtful whether a fit rider would have mattered too much. Only Jack Milne, the fast-gating American, provided any threat to the Aces and deserved more than the 12 points he amassed. Again the heavy scoring of Kitchen and Langton guided the Aces towards glory, with a dream final against Wembley beckoning, as the Lions had dispatched Southampton from the competition.

George Pepper of Newcastle, always a popular visitor to Manchester.

That dream was to be shattered within a matter of days. The Belle Vue Aces had, in fact, ridden the last senior meeting at Hyde Road prior to hostilities breaking out. However, it was not the last track action as Bristol appeared on Wednesday 30 August, in the National Provincial Trophy semi-final for Division Two sides. Belle Vue II made great strides towards the final, winning 66-29. Confidence oozed as Ernie Price posted a faultless score and was ably assisted by Tommy Bateman and Alan Butler. Ernie had the distinction of winning the Flying Twelve Final, which was the last pre-war race to take place at the stadium. The second leg was cancelled due to the crisis in Europe, as were all other meetings. When speedway racing would be seen again was anybody's guess. The Aces were scheduled to ride at home to Southampton on 2 September. Although this match was cancelled, a small number of programmes for the meeting have appeared over the years.

It would be wrong to speculate who may have won the outstanding league titles and cups. Certainly, Belle Vue headed the table at the cessation of racing. However, the claims of Wimbledon and Wembley could not be ignored as any slip up by Belle Vue may have paved the way for either team. Belle Vue II themselves may have contested a cup final. Who knows what might have happened!

THE WAR YEARS

The final and most glorious chapter in this era came after war was declared in September 1939. It was expected that speedway racing would cease, but no, not even war could beat Belle Vue! The wartime speedway meetings held at Hyde Road hold a unique place in the sport's history. These exploits will probably never be surpassed, as Belle Vue continued to entertain supporters throughout the war. Having been the dominant force in domestic competitions during the 1933-1937 period, Belle Vue now took on perhaps its most daunting challenge of all. After all, the idea of staging sporting events was to boost the morale of the people. In these dark days, the citizens of Manchester appreciated the efforts of the club. Programmes, including the famous *Belle Vue Bulletin*, were issued every meeting. It was not unusual for these to be sold out because of the limited numbers printed due to a paper shortage. As ever, racing started promptly at 7p.m., but some early and late season meetings had a 6.45p.m. start time. Even grading the track between races was dispensed with – the reason being there was not enough fuel to run the tractor.

The Belle Vue management's concern was not solely the speedway. They also did their bit towards the war effort. A facility was given within the Belle Vue Gardens to the St John Ambulance for people to give blood. At the speedway meetings, people were encouraged to attend the station and make their contribution. This was run in conjunction with the Manchester Blood Transfusion Campaign.

Many riders were left disappointed by last minute hitches with their arrangements. Tommy Price, of Wembley, was a typical example. He was ready to journey to Manchester for the evening meeting, only to get a last minute call from the Air Ministry to report at once. Finally arriving in Manchester, Price was only able to take a couple of rides.

From 23 September 1939 to 20 October 1945, Belle Vue staged weekly race meetings and not one was ever postponed or incomplete. Towards the end the war Alice Hart, who was now in charge, began to use the meetings as training sessions. She could see that once the hostilities had ceased, league speedway would return. A few of the Aces pre-war stars would not return to

Eric Langton.

Manchester and replacements would be needed.

The speedway purchased bikes for the visiting riders to use if needed. A supply of fuel (not petrol) had always been kept at Hyde Road and this proved vital to the successful running of wartime speedway. Wilf Plant had three bikes that were left at Belle Vue and, on one particular evening, poor Wilf ended up having no bike to ride himself as he had loaned out all three to others, who were in the same race as him!

The first official wartime meeting was ridden on 23 September, when teams led by Frank Varey and Eric Langton met in a challenge. Langton's team won the encounter by 69-39. The scores from that first meeting were as follows:

Eric Langton	17	Frank Varey	15
Alan Butler	4	Tommy Bateman	2
Bob Harrison	14	Joe Abbott	9
Oliver Hart	9	Jack Gordon	1
Oliver Langton	10	Jack Hargreaves	6
Ernie Price	13	Ted Bravery	6
Harold Jackson	2	Walter Hull	did not ride
Jack White	did not ride	'Acorn' Dobson	did not ride

Harold Jackson leads Oliver Hart and Jack White on 20 April 1940.

Paddy Mills on leave.

The second and last meeting of 1939 was on 30 September. Nobody knew at this time how any future meetings would be composed. A date for the grand reopening was announced as 22 March 1940. Racing during the war presented many problems to the organisers. A meeting could only be held in daylight hours. Any meeting that was incomplete before darkness fell would have to be curtailed, although this never happened.

Perhaps Belle Vue's biggest headache was the availability of the most essential item – the riders! Miss Hart could never be absolutely sure who was going to turn up. A rider would agree to turn up, but not be able to when the time came. In general, the majority of the riders were stationed around the Lancashire area or had reasonable access to Manchester. No rider who turned up would be refused rides. Some arrived only to find that there were no places available, but they would be accommodated the following week. Riders like Tommy Allott, Jack White and Ernie Appleby would turn up every week, but Belle Vue had an agreement that they would drop out to allow riders who had travelled a distance to race.

The early meetings in 1940 consisted of a composite Belle Vue team riding against other made up teams such as Harringay, Glasgow White City, West Ham, Wembley and The Rest. This type of meeting was gradually phased out in favour of individual and pairs events. Belle Vue did manage one 'away' meeting against Glasgow on 8 May 1940; they lost by 43-40. Although the teams were not a true representation of a particular club, it has to be remembered that the main aim was to provide entertainment for the public.

Above left: *Stan Williams, Belle Vue 1940.* Above right: *Bill Kitchen on leave.* Left: *Captain Eric W Gregory.*

Probably the most prestigious meeting during the war was the British Individual Championship. The 1940 final took place on 10 August and ended with Bill Kitchen, Eric Langton and Eric Chitty tying in first place. A series of two-rider match races between the three riders were used to determine the champion. Eric Chitty won the series to become the first wartime British Champion.

Previously it has been mentioned that riders could never be certain whether or not they would be available. Bill Kitchen took steps to ensure that he would be available for most meetings. He was stationed in the south during 1940 but preferred being closer to home. He applied to be relocated in his native Lancashire and Bill was in luck. Someone in the north had made a request to go south and, as they were doing the same job, an exchange was arranged. This ensured that he would be able to appear at Belle Vue most weeks. Bill did miss a few Saturdays by having to assist with the garage at Galgate.

The club gave the fans everything they wanted. They arranged for a double bill of racing on Whit and August Bank Holiday Mondays in 1941. Afternoon and evening meetings were staged on both these holiday dates and proved popular with the supporters. Seeing the same riders week after week presented no problems to the spectators. They appreciated the lengths that riders would take to entertain them. It gave them a chance to forget the constant threat from Europe. Crowds were very good, although they were not 'full houses'. This justified Belle Vue running these weekly meetings.

In 1942, Belle Vue held a meeting called the Victory Trophy. Mr Victor Martin had donated the trophy, together with a replica to the club. Supporters were to have a chance of winning the replica; each of the programmes was numbered and a draw conducted during the interval. Programmes were in short supply and sold out well before the start time.

George Pepper DFC, who had ridden many times for Newcastle against Belle Vue, was killed in an aircraft accident. He and his co-pilot were known as the 'Perfect Team'. Pepper was Canadian and came to England as a TT representative. He ended up having trials at West Ham on Eric Chitty's recommendation and was made captain of Newcastle in 1938. His appearances in wartime meetings had been limited and his passing came as a shock to everyone.

Complimentary season tickets.

VOL. 16 **522nd MEETING** **No. 8**

SATURDAY, JUNE 5th, 1943

At 7-0 P.M.

No. **3451**

BELLE VUE
PROGRAMME

NO PETROL WHATSOEVER
USED AT THESE MEETINGS

PRICE **6**^D PRICE

ALL MEETINGS UNDER THE
AUSPICES OF THE NORTH
MANCHESTER MOTOR CLUB

ISSUED EVERY WEEK

Typical 1940s programme cover.

For the remainder of the war, speedway continued to be a popular diversion with Manchester folk, who flocked each week for the excitement. The organisation of meetings, however, still caused problems. Things did become easier by 1945, as riders who had served their country began returning to Britain. There was still the curfew on when meetings had to be finished, but this was never imposed, as racing was always over within the stipulated constraints.

In 1945, the Belle Vue training school began to bear fruit. Alice Hart arranged six meetings, specifically for novice riders. These were ridden on Wednesday evenings in June and July. Admission to the events was 9d (4p), which included entry to all parts of the stadium. The budding stars, all wanting to break into the big time, were given something meaningful to race for. Six senior riders donated the prizes in the form of trophies. To win the Eric Langton or Frank Varey Trophy was a feather in the cap for these lads. A young man called Dent Oliver became the star pupil. He was the outstanding novice rider and met with a good deal of success. Dent was a protégé of Bob Harrison and had not ridden on cinders at all until he registered with the training school.

An amazing 170 senior meetings took place during the war period; in addition, there were the six 'All Novice' events. The arrangement and running of these meetings in a period of hostility was a marvellous achievement. This bears testament to the determination of Alice Hart, together with other officials, not to allow evil to triumph over good. Crowds could not attend in the pre-war numbers, but as life became easier in 1945, the supporters returned and several 30,000 crowds were recorded.

Frank Varey finally announced his retirement from racing, but the Red Devil was not

Ron Johnson leads Eric Langton.

Above: *Eric Gregory passes Oliver Hart.* Below: *Eric Gregory, leads Oliver Hart and Frank Varey, with Fred Tuck trailing.*

Above: *Eric Gregory trails Norman Evans, Wilf Plant and Tommy Allott.* Right: *Frank Varey at the end of a glorious career.*

lost to the sport. He opted to become the promoter at Owlerton, Sheffield, where three meetings were held in late 1945. His retirement was short-lived. Finding that there was a vacant place, Frank ended his riding exile and somehow managed a disqualification in his first race.

Two riders, who would have served Belle Vue well in the post-war years, were denied the chance when fate intervened. Jack Hargreaves had a glittering career ahead of him at Belle Vue. His first rides came in 1934 and, inside two years, he was riding for Liverpool. By 1937 Jack had realised his ambition, to ride for the Aces. He was partnered with Eric Langton, who took him under his wing. Hargreaves made rapid progress and, by 1938, he was holding down a regular team place. Throughout the hostilities, he worked at his wartime job, but never failed to answer the call when asked to appear in Manchester. Sadly, on 15 January 1944, Jack was involved in a fatal accident when his bike was in a collision with a bus, on his way home from work. Maurice Butler was an aspiring novice in 1945, Belle Vue's second most important find after Dent Oliver. His pals and the supporters referred to him as 'Young' Butler. His elder brother, Alan, an ex-Aces asset, had built a special machine for him. On 22 August 1945, Butler fell heavily after clipping the back wheel of an opponent. He sustained slight concussion and a few bruises, but gave no reason to be concerned. After Maurice and other members of his family had set off home, he became unconscious and was taken to hospital in Birmingham. He was operated on but never came out of the anaesthetic. A ruptured main artery caused the death of this promising rider.

The four-lap, clutch start track record stood at 73.4 seconds after the final meeting of 1945. Norman Parker set the time on 27 May 1944, during the Grand Prix meeting, which he won when paired with Eric Chitty.

To complete the War Years, the winners of the principal events held are shown below.

British Individual Champion

1940	Eric Chitty
1941	Eric Chitty
1942	Eric Chitty
1943	Ron Clarke
1944	Frank Varey
1945	Bill Kitchen

Northern Champion

1940	Bill Kitchen
1941	Oliver Hart
1942	Eric Chitty
1943	Norman Parker
1944	Norman Parker
1945	Alec Statham

All England Best Pairs

1940	Eric Langton-Frank Varey
1941	Ron Johnson-Eric Chitty
1942	Bill Kitchen-Oliver Hart
1943	Eric Chitty-Fred Tuck
1944	Competition not held
1945	Ron Johnson-Alec Statham

Belle Vue Grand Prix

1940	Eric Langton-Frank Varey (tied)
1941	Bill Kitchen
1942	Eric Chitty
1943	Norman Parker
1944	Norman Parker
1945	Tommy Price

Empire Best Pairs

1941	Eric Langton-Frank Varey
	Bill Kitchen-Oliver Hart (tied)
1942	Frank Varey-Bill Kitchen
1943	Bill Kitchen-Oliver Hart
1944	Eric Chitty-Ron Clarke
1945	Jack Parker-Bill Pitcher

Belle Vue Speedway Derby

1940	Jack Parker
1941	Frank Varey
1942	Bill Longley
1943	Competition not held
1944	Norman Parker
1945	Jack Parker-Tommy Price (Pairs)

A tribute to the men who kept Belle Vue speedway alive.

The riders who kept the flag flying during the dark days of the war are given below, even those who only rode in a few meetings. Without them, this special period in Belle Vue speedway's long existence could never have taken place. Their exploits gained them legendary status within the sport and a permanent place in Belle Vue's history.

Eric Langton
Oliver Hart
Jack Hargreaves
Fred Tuck
Bill Kitchen
Ernie Appleby
Bill Pitcher
Les Wotton
Ron Clarke
Tommy Price
Morian Hansen
Malcolm Craven

Frank Varey
Oliver Langton
Ernie Price
Wilf Plant
Joe Abbott
Jack Parker
Norman Parker
Alec Statham
Eric Chitty
Eric Gregory
George Wilks
Ron Johnson

Bill Longley
Wally Lloyd
Wal Morton
Tommy Allott
Doug McClachlan
Stan Dell
Phil Hart
Norman Evans
George Pepper
Dicky Wise
Paddy Mills
Stan Williams

Belle Vue Speedway League Record 1929-1939

	Year	Matches	Won	Drawn	Lost	For	Against	Points	League
*	1929	10	6		4	332.0	288.0	12	English DT League (withdrew)
	1930	21	19	1	1	451.5	290.5	39	Northern League
	1931	18	12		6	528.0	426.0	24	Northern League
**	1931	38	14		24	916.0	1,091.0	28	Southern League
	1932	18	11		7	548.0	411.0	22	NPA Competition
	1932	16	9	1	6	448.5	397.5	19	National League
	1933	36	31		5	1,358.5	888.5	62	National League
	1934	32	27		5	1,040.0	650.0	54	National League One
	1934	12	3		9	174.0	240.0	6	National League Two
	1935	24	18	2	4	957.0	752.0	38	National League
	1936	24	18	1	5	971.0	733.0	37	National League
	1937	24	13		11	1,094.0	909.0	26	National League
***	1937	20	8		12	774.0	883.0	16	Provincial League
	1938	24	11		13	949.0	1,052.0	22	National League
*****	1939	16	12	1	3	762.0	575.0	25	National League One
*****	1939	14	4		10	490.0	678.0	8	National League Two
		347	216	6	125	11,793.5	10,264.5	438	

* The first result found has been used, although there several variations known to some matches

** Took over the fixtures of Harringay

*** Took over the fixtures of Liverpool

**** As at the outbreak of war

***** Took over Stoke fixtures and shows the position at the outbreak of war

THE ROLL OF HONOUR

Belle Vue Speedway 1928-45

1928
Opened on 28 July by International Speedways Limited. Meetings held at the Greyhound Stadium, Kirkmanshulme Lane, Gorton. Racing consisted of individual events.

1929
Opened on 23 March under the auspices of the North Manchester Motor Club at the Belle Vue Sports Ground, Hyde Road, Gorton. Members of the English Dirt Track League, but withdrew in July.

1930
Members of the Northern League. Finished as champions.

1931
Members of the Northern League. Finished as champions and cup winners.

1931
Invited to enter a team in the Southern League under the name of Manchester, after the withdrawal of Harringay. Finished 8th.

1932
Members of the National League. Finished 4th and were runners up in the *Daily Mail* National Trophy.

1933
Members of the National League. Finished as champions. Winners of the *Daily Mail* National Trophy.

1934
Members of the National League. Finished as champions. Winners of the *Daily Mail* National Trophy and the ACU Cup.

1934
Members of the National League Second Division. Finished 6th.

1935
Members of the National League. Finished as champions. Winners of the *Daily Mail* National Trophy and the ACU Cup.

1936
Members of the National League. Finished as champions. Winners of the *Daily Mail* National Trophy and the ACU Cup.

1937
Members of the National League. Finished 4th. Winners of the *Daily Mail* National Trophy and the ACU Cup.

1937
Took over the fixtures of Liverpool in July, in the Provincial League. Finished 4th.

1938
Members of the National League. Finished 5th.

1938
Entered Belle Vue II in the National League Second Division. The team was based at Sheffield, but eventually participated in cup matches only. Winners of the English Cup.

1939
Members of the National League. Top of the league at the outbreak of war. Finalists in the *Daily Mail* National Trophy and winners of the British Speedway Cup (formerly The ACU Cup).

1939
Took over the fixtures of Stoke in June, in the National League Second Division. Last place at the outbreak of war.

TRACK RECORDS AS AT 20 OCTOBER 1945

Four Lap Standing Start	E. Chitty	77.0	22/04/44
Four Lap Flying Start	J. Parker	72.0	14/07/45
Four Lap Clutch Start	N. Parker	73.4	27/05/44
Lancashire Mile (Flying Start)	J. Abbott	78.6	14/04/34
Four Lap Car Record (Flying Start)	W. Mackereth	76.0	31/08/38
Lap Record (Flying Start)	E. Langton	17.8	12/08/37
Lap Record (Clutch Start)	V. Huxley	20.0	18/05/35
Side Car Lap Record (Flying Start)	G. Richards	22.4	04/07/31
Two Lap Dash Record (Flying Start)	E. Chitty	36.0	11/08/45

3

AUDENSHAW

1928

Meetings at Audenshaw Speedway were held sporadically, but, despite this, they led a very troubled existence. Disputes with the racing authorities, the riders and other smaller groups all played significant parts. Sadly, fatalities weighed heavily on the organisers' shoulders. On the plus side, spectators saw some spectacular and fast racing. There were, also, one or two light hearted moments to lift flagging spirits.

The Audenshaw Racecourse, situated directly behind the Snipe Inn on Ashton Old Road, staged the second dirt-track event in Manchester on Saturday 3 March 1928. Prior to this meeting, the racecourse had been used solely for Horse Trotting Races. It was situated a quarter of a mile away from the site of the old Droylsden track, across the Ashton Moss. Cinders were used to form the base of the track, which had an official measurement of half a mile and 2 inches. Each bend had a width ranging from 40 to 50 feet and straights measuring a minimum of 32 feet.

Racing was to be conducted under the auspices of the South Manchester Motor Club, on Racing Permit No R105. Entry forms were available to would-be competitors, giving details of club regulations and prize money on offer. Two of the club's competitors' marshals were to go in opposite directions during the ensuing seasons. Norman Jackman went on to be the popular speedway manager at Farringdon Park, Preston, in 1929, while James Wolfenden was associated with several ventures, but, more importantly, he was part of the promotion when racing ceased in 1931.

Two Australians, Billy Galloway and Keith Mackay, were billed as the main attractions for demonstration races of the sensational new sport. Galloway, in fact, toured Audenshaw and the surrounding districts to advertise the forthcoming event. The South Manchester Motor Club was determined not to fall foul of a lack of publicity. Fortunately for them, the impact of the High Beech meeting, when an estimated 30,000 turned up, was still fresh in the public's mind. Mackay had practised on the new circuit but was not entirely happy with the surface, which had been rolled heavily, making the art of 'broadsiding' difficult. However, he was happy with the general condition of the circuit.

When the big day arrived, sixty-five entries had been approved. Several of these, namely Alec Jackson, Harry Riley 'Ginger' Lees, Bob Harrison, Walter Hull, Stanley 'Acorn' Dobson and Tommy Price (Liverpool and Preston), were to become household names over the next few years. A crowd of 20,000 packed into the racecourse. Racing started at 2 p.m. and it was not long before the first crash happened. The incident occurred when Harrison attempted a full-blooded broadside around the outside, only to take a heavy tumble into the fence. Thankfully, he was just shaken up. Some of the

SOUTH MANCHESTER MOTOR CLUB

AFFILIATED TO THE A.C.U. THROUGH THE NORTH WESTERN CENTRE.

ANNOUNCE A

DIRT TRACK RACE MEETING

ON A LARGER SCALE THAN HAS EVER BEEN PRODUCED.

A Restricted Race Meeting held under the General Competition Rules of the A.C.U., by virtue of Permit No. R105 issued by the A.C.U., North Western Centre, and Supplementary Regulations contained herein.

A Member of any Club affiliated to the North-Western Centre (A.C.U.) can compete in this event.

TO BE HELD AT

AUDENSHAW RACECOURSE,

Ashton Old Road, Audenshaw, Manchester,

On Saturday, March 3rd, 1928, at 2 p.m.

The whole interest of the Motor Cycling world is focused on this class of event.

Steward of the Meeting: A. HOGGART (S.M.M.C.).
Timekeeper: A.C.U. TIMEKEEPER.

Here is a glorious opportunity for you to become acquainted with this class of Racing, shortly to be specialized in by our Colonial Visitors.

☛ OVER £50 IN PRIZES.

AWARDS.

3 SOLID GOLD WATCHES (15 Jewelled Movement), value £7/10/- each.
6 CANTEENS OF CUTLERY, value £3/10/- each.
6 SOLID SILVER CIGARETTE CASES, value £1/10/- each.

In departing from the usual practice of presenting Cups and Medals for more useful and valuable awards, we are quite prepared to award Cups of same value if the winners so desire.

PRACTISING WILL BE ALLOWED ON SATURDAY, MARCH 3rd, from 12 to 1 p.m.

An advertisement for Audenshaw's opening meeting.

Programme cover of Audenshaw's opening meeting.

crowd, around 400, decided that they needed a better view of racing and climbed onto the stand roof. People standing below noticed that the beams were beginning to sag. Officials and the police persuaded the offenders to come down, thus avoiding a potential disaster. Meanwhile, keenly fought races and a few spills thrilled the crowd. Keith Mackay triumphed in the Winners versus Australians race, when engine trouble forced Galloway to retire.

Overall, everything went to plan; spectators left the stadium pleased with the racing and eagerly looking forward to the next meeting. Altogether six further events were arranged, with the last one taking place on 19 May. There was also a change in ownership. The British Dirt Track Racing Association (BDTRA), which was Manchester-based, took over the running of the speedway on an Open Racing Permit.

During this period of inactivity, measures were taken to improve security and change the nature of the track. After the scare when people sat on the roof, precautions were taken to ensure that this would not happen again. Galloway and Mackay suggested that the cinders, although smooth, had been packed down too hard and that a loose surface would help considerably. Tons of loose cinders were laid and smoothed out. At a practice session, local riders gave it their approval. The track perimeter had a wire fence erected. It has to be said that the association did listen to constructive ideas, which, sadly, did not happen in future seasons.

'Ginger' Lees was the star of the second meeting. He won all of his qualifying races and the finals of the 350 and 500 cc class. For his efforts, Lees won £60 in prize money, quite a sum for an afternoon's work! Despite it being an ideal day for racing, the attendance of 10,000 came as a disappointment, but perhaps the eight-week break had something to do with this. Lees' winning streak came to an end the following week. He found it difficult to stay on his bike and was lucky to finish second in the final, after falling off and remounting. Peter Waterhouse and Norman Hartley were less fortunate. Waterhouse took a heavy fall, resulting in a broken collarbone. Hartley flipped over his handlebars and landed on his head, suffering concussion. The spectators were, by now, learning that there was a more serious side to speedway. Whenever a rider fell, a hush came over the crowd, until they could see their favourite get up again. To show that age was not a barrier, local motorcyclist George 'Pa' Cowley took part and he was sixty-eight years old.

Ever more demanding, the big Audenshaw following wanted to see more star men.

Stewie St George.

The organisers booked Stewie St George as an attraction and were rewarded with a 10,000 attendance for the afternoon meeting. St George had little difficulty in defeating his local rivals to win the Audenshaw Cup. Curious to see if two meetings in one day would be a success, an extra evening event took place. Although racing was of a high quality, the crowd was low and this convinced the organisers not to repeat this. Races varied between five and ten laps and some took over six minutes to complete the course.

Light Car Races were arranged as a variation for what turned out to be the final meeting of 1928. Torrential rain spoiled the proceedings and even the cars had difficulty in finishing races. Surface water played havoc with the riders' engines, resulting in many breakdowns. Arthur Franklyn was the outstanding rider of the day and fully deserved his win in the main final. The BDTRA was disappointed with the low crowd of 5,000. Prior to the start, it was announced that further meetings would be arranged after the Isle of Man TT races. In reality, this brought a premature end to the 1928 season.

1929

When the Stalybridge Motor Club took over the ownership, it ended the speculation that speedway at Audenshaw would not happen in 1929. There was a problem with the Northern Association of Dirt Track Owners (NADTO), who were the driving force behind the newly formed English Dirt Track League in the North of England. They would not admit Audenshaw into the association. In a further twist to the tale, Audenshaw reached an agreement to interchange riders with Belle Vue, who were, coincidentally, members of the NADTO. This plan met the approval of the ACU, which had already issued licence No. 283 and Permit No. TA55 to the track. However, the Stalybridge Motor Club refused to be put off and were determined to carry on with the planned schedule.

Alterations had been made to the track and amenities. There had been a fence on the infield, but this did cause problems for riders wanting to leave the circuit. Having it removed gave easier and safer access to the centre green. The cinder track surface had not been in very good condition. This was rectified, to the satisfaction of the riders.

Despite the problems, the season started on 25 May with the usual individual events. Belle Vue star, Arthur Franklyn, who was the main attraction, had little difficulty in winning the Puritan Cup and prize money of £25. One of the problems throughout the season was the lower than expected attendance. Again, as with the previous year, Stewie St George was booked to appear. His all-action style usually thrilled spectators, but he met with no success on this visit. His chances were ruined by two falls when in a favourable position. Sidecar events were also used to try and tempt the missing numbers back. However, the introduction of demonstration car races proved so popular, it was decided to apply for a licence to run permanent car events.

Much to the annoyance of the NADTO, certain riders continued appearing despite warnings. In retaliation, bans from appearing on any affiliated tracks were given out. This did not seem to bother anyone, the situation remained as before and the riders simply kept on turning up. What the association did not seem to grasp was that most of the Audenshaw riders could earn more by operating outside their jurisdiction. In effect, they were freelance riders and were able to negotiate higher rates than the ones offered by the association. Far from receiving the backing of member tracks, the NADTO had to deal with unhappy promoters, who were now unable to utilise the banned riders. Suggestions that some tracks could break away in the near future became a distinct possibility. Belle Vue was one of these affected, due to their close ties with Audenshaw.

For the first time, fully masked riders appeared in attempts to conceal their identity. Rumours abounded as to who they actually were. It was common knowledge that they were well-known dirt-track stars. They were riding simply because they could earn far more than plying their trade with 'legal' promotions. Noms de plume were used by the men. Assumed names like Pentonville, Strangeways and Dartmoor blended in to the situation of racing at an unrecognised speedway track.

Tragedy occurred on 18 June, when George Rowlands became the first rider to be killed at Audenshaw. After the second race of the Flying Nine, Larry Coffey had the unpleasant task of informing the hushed crowd that Rowlands had died from his injuries. Racing was abandoned as a mark of respect. The incident happened in the junior heat when Rowlands slid into the bend, lost control and fell. Lord, the rider immediately behind, broke his leg after smashing into the fence. George Rowlands was not so lucky; he received a blow to the forehead from Lord's bike and was carried unconscious from the scene. The stricken riders were taken to the ambulance room. Lord was transported to hospital, but, sadly, Rowlands passed away from his terrible injuries. A verdict of accidental death was returned at the inquest. Arthur Franklyn, the Belle Vue star, was a witness. He was of the opinion that the track surface was consistent.

The coroner made the following recommendations to Audenshaw and the ACU: Riders were to wear adequate protective clothing. All riders were to hold a licence and juniors wishing to hold a licence would have to pass an ability test. Juniors and seniors should not compete against each other. This should be enforced by the ACU. Races should not have more than four riders. The track should be kept in good repair before and during meetings.

Three further meetings took place after Rowlands's death. There should have been a fourth on 2 July, but this was cancelled owing to a lack of available water due to the

The final resting place of George Rowlands, who was killed in 1929.

very hot spell. To boost its crowds, Audenshaw's promotion booked three American riders, who proved great entertainers. 'Red' Murch, 'Chick' Remington and 'Dab' Boston stood head and shoulders above the other racers. Considering their limited experience of English conditions, they acquitted themselves well. It took time for a sense of normality to return, but the crowds improved slightly and the racing was exciting. A sudden suspension of racing caught everyone by surprise. The Stalybridge Motor Club had run into financial difficulties. This gave no option but to cease racing. Their intention was to re-open again in around three weeks' time, but this did not come about. Part of the problem had been very dusty meetings, caused by a totally inadequate watering system. The track only had a very small water cart and, in extremely hot weather, it had little or no effect.

It became apparent the motor club would not be able carry on, due to the financial constraints. Fortunately, a new promotion, the Northern Motor Sports Ltd, under the auspices once again of the South Manchester Motor Club, reached an amicable agreement for the rights to run the speedway. Before the formal signing of the takeover could take place, recognition by the NADTO had to be applied for. For their part, the association realised that it was not in their best interests to keep the previous suspensions in place. Therefore, these were lifted, allowing the riders to race at any track in the Manchester area. In the meantime, Belle Vue, who had previously voiced their dissatisfaction with the association, withdrew from the English Dirt Track League but they were not the only dissenters.

A crowd of about 6,000 welcomed speedway back on 10 August. The riders were mostly the same as before. There were, however, one or two new names to Audenshaw. Norman Dawson, who had been the captain of the ill-fated Bolton Speedway, rode to victory in the Palatine Cup. Arthur Franklyn suffered all night with machine trouble and failed to impress the crowds. Once again, sidecars were used as an alternative.

The following week, the promotion went for quality. Apart from the early meetings, the big names had not been used, but, having the likes of Frank Charles, Dicky Wise and Cliff Watson riding, it did show that Audenshaw wanted to put on a top class event. Their enterprise was rewarded with bad luck. Heavy rain on race day saturated the track and made passing difficult. The inclement conditions also affected the attendance, with only 4,000 braving the rain. Charles made light of the muddy surface; a spectacular burst of speed propelling him beyond rivals Watson and Wise, to win the coveted Golden Helmet. The appearance of Albert Brendan Drew in the South Manchester Handicap final gave the crowd a new hero. Although Mark Sheldon won the race, Albert pushed Sheldon all the way and eventually had to settle for third place after oversliding on the final lap. Affectionately christened 'Abel' by the crowd, Drew was a true entertainer and was destined to be a prominent figure in future seasons.

The 1929 season ended on 7 September, when Salford-based rider Sid Newiss won the Golden Helmet, gaining a narrow win from the Rochdale star, 'Squib' Burton. Earlier, Burton had managed to defeat Norman Dawson in a best of three race challenge. Before this final meeting, rainy weather had affected the previous meetings' racing and attendances, which were particularly low. Curtailing racing at this juncture was taken from a business point of view. To continue could well have resulted in further financial problems.

1930

If it was thrills, spills and controversy that you were looking for, then Audenshaw certainly was the place to be. The 1930 season was the most successful of the four seasons held there. The track was not in its best condition, crowds being consistently higher than any previous seasons, but there was controversy before and throughout the season. The new promotion, The Manchester Motor Sports Club, had been looking at staging racing on Sundays. This certainly stirred feelings in many different ways. Sporting events had, for many years, been frowned upon because of the Sunday Observance Act. However, there was legally nothing that could be done to prevent this happening. Other Manchester tracks would not arrange Sunday meetings as they were under the control of the ACU, which were unhappy with the situation. Again they warned riders of the consequences, saying that bans would be imposed on any participating rider. This was as a result of the promotion breaking away from the ACU.

On the day of the opening meeting, 25,000 spectators attended. Much of the interest was over the breaking of the Observance Act and whether any action would be taken at the meeting by the ACU. It is thought that only 15,000 gained access by paying. Police officers were on duty to control the traffic on Manchester Road, but there were none inside the grounds. People were still arriving after a few races had been run. Suddenly, groups who had gathered outside forced open a few gates, resulting in thousands flooding through, with officials attempting in vain to stem the tide. There was obviously not enough room around the perimeter of the track, so they proceeded to run across the circuit and sit on the grassy infield.

Racing was suspended because of the spectators being too close to the bends. The clerk of the course, James Wolfenden, persuaded them to move back to a safe distance. Things settled down and the remainder of the afternoon passed without further mishap, until the last event. Car racing was to have taken place but had to be abandoned when the crowd declined to leave the centre. The promotion had planned further meetings, but they had to look at their safety procedures, in order to prevent a repetition of the dangerous behaviour of an element of the crowd.

Complaints about Sunday racing were arriving at the speedway offices and also at the local council. Naturally, the church was the most vehement voice. They, and the council, thought that, in the meantime, a resolution of protest should be given to the Audenshaw promoters. However, it would really have had little effect on them. They would point to the fact that with so many attending the meeting, there was justification to continue. One councillor gave a quote, stating that 'Audenshaw, if it is permitted to continue, could become a second Sodom and Gomorrah.' (*Ashton Reporter*, June 1930.)

During the month of June, the Audenshaw promoter, James Wolfenden, made attempts to take on another track. This was at Raikes Park, Bolton, where speedway had previously been held in 1928 and 1929. Terms could not be agreed with the stadium landlords and the idea was shelved.

A rare image depicting Sid Meadowcroft getting to his feet at Audenshaw in 1929.

Although the scenes from the previous week were not repeated, the repercussions certainly were and the crowd was down to around 10,000. Former policemen assisted with crowd control. 'Abel' Drew and 'Riskit' Riley again provided the thrills, but it was the exhibition races between two ladies that captured the crowd's imagination. Far from interfering with Audenshaw's business, the ACU bans actually created interest, with applications to ride arriving daily. Several years ago, Peter Waterhouse, who competed at Audenshaw, described the track in 1930 as being a speedy one and very smooth. Perhaps, with it being so big, it was too fast, which is why injuries from high-speed crashes were commonplace. Riders were literally flying into the wide, open bends and it was usually the inexperienced riders who piled up. He also revealed the real names of some of the noms de plume. Maybe they were not famous names, but as they also raced in other types of ACU events, it was important to remain anonymous. The following are some of these.

Real Name	Nom de Plume
Peter Waterhouse	A. Pedro
Tom Kenny	Billy Brown
Jim Kenny	Jack Smith
Charles Deakin	Dan de Lyon
Fred Ibbotson	Slider Jones
Frank Partington	MacDonald

Overall, the promotion flourished. Racing was, as always, keenly contested. Crucially, new young riders began to make their mark. Billy Brown and Dan de Lyon were the emerging stars of Audenshaw, both brave riders, but Dan, in particular, was a bit reckless. They were not afraid to push themselves and their opponents to the limit. With the July weather being extremely hot, the track needed to be dampened down. Unfortunately, the watering system was inadequate and resulted in clouds of dust impairing the view of spectators. Steps were taken to remedy this, by installing pipes around the outside of the track. As luck would have it, the first meeting when they could be utilised was disrupted by heavy rain. A meagre crowd of 4,000 turned up to watch a lacklustre meeting.

The 3 August meeting took place in front of 15,000, who, on this occasion, paid for admission. Surprisingly, the majority of the crowd came from Ashton-under-Lyne, from where most of the complaints about Sunday racing had been received. A different type of race format was adopted, with an Inter City match between Salford and Manchester. Salford won by 13-11. Prior to this meeting, there had been a slight track problem with bumps and ruts appearing. Having noted these, the management returned the track to a reasonable condition. Torrential rain affected the following week's meeting, turning the track into a quagmire. Abandoning the meeting was the only option; racing in these conditions would be farcical for riders and spectators alike.

Other forms of entertainment were being considered, especially for during the interval. Local brass bands seemed to be a reasonable idea, but when donkey racing was suggested, it created problems on the grounds of health. Should a rider fall and sustain an open wound, infection by various diseases could occur. On a lighter note, some locals wanted to know if the donkeys would be wearing helmets during races!

On 17 August, a crowd of 17,000 flocked to the meeting, resulting in the highest paying attendance of the season. The principal event of the afternoon was The Matrimonial Stakes between teams of single and married men. Dan de Lyon surprised everyone when he won his first race. He fell heavily, but not only managed to remount his bike, he sped after the others and passed them in a thrilling finish. Needless to say, this brought the house down. Dan was, by now, a big hero with both young and old spectators. Billy Brown was also quietly making a name for himself. Not many weeks went by without Brown being one of the finalists.

It was at this meeting that spectators were injured. Two children, who were standing close to the mesh fencing, received leg cuts when Dean parted company with his machine. Dean was thrown into the air, before falling on the track. His bike went into the fence, injuring the children, who received minor treatment at the track.

Everything seemed to be going smoothly when, on 31 August, tragedy struck again. William Owen, from Widnes, had aspirations to become a dirt-track star. Owen really wanted to race at his local track in Warrington. Rides there were not forthcoming, so he decided to try his luck at Audenshaw, but found progression difficult. He was persuaded by his parents to give up racing. An acceptable offer for his machine was received, but, for whatever reason, he decided to honour the booking from Audenshaw. Owen was a front marker in the Audenshaw Handicap. He was racing at speed down the back straight, when he broadsided into the bend to decelerate and he lost control. A hole had appeared in the track, he hit this and was pitched over the handlebars before landing heavily. 'Slider' Shuttleworth hit the fence to avoid an

Austin Humphries a regular at Audenshaw.

accident, but it was another rider who collided with Owen. The crowd could see that it was a serious injury and watched silently as Owen was conveyed to hospital. It was only after the meeting had ended that news of the rider's death reached the promoters.

At the inquest, a number of witnesses confirmed the presence of potholes in the track. The inference was that the track maintenance fell below safety standards. The entry to one of the bends was not in a poor condition. When an ACU official was asked why a licence had not been granted to Audenshaw, the reply was that no application had been received. Another complaint was that the fence did not have any spring in it and could be pushed up to the piping that spectators leant against. The coroner, who had attended a meeting to see speedway himself, was happy to allow racing to continue, despite calls to close the track. He asked for the condition of the track surface and the fence to be looked at. Also he recommended that spectators be kept at a safe distance from the fence.

One September meeting had a delayed start due to a riders' strike. It seemed that the riders were still on the same pay rates applicable from the opening day of the 1930 season. As the crowds had been reasonably high, some riders, with the backing of the NADTO, decided to approach the management and negotiate new rates. The association was affiliated to the ACU and the promotion felt that there was some pressure being put on them by certain riders. The meeting went ahead after an agreement was reached, although the problem resurfaced after the meeting.

Crowds gradually dwindled after the death of William Owen. By the time the season had ended the attendance had fallen by almost 75 per cent. Although this disappointed the promotion, racing continued, up to 26 October.

Four meetings were completed in October in front of around 6,000 – a stark contrast to the season's opening event. Even a charity meeting for the Ashton Infirmary failed to inspire a larger following. During the final weeks, racing was not very eventful. Poor attendance made the promotion rethink the idea of holding a meeting over the festive holidays. If they could only attract meagre crowds now, what chance would they have in the middle of winter?

Over the season covering eighteen meetings, Audenshaw paid out prize money totalling £1,900, together with the trophies.

1931

When the speedway season began in May 1931, the ultimate closure of Audenshaw was the furthest thought in spectators' minds. A spell of bad weather affected the opening meetings and also kept the crowds down. Appearing on the Audenshaw scene for the first time were a trio of colourful characters called 'The Thriller', 'The Red Terror' and 'Anzac'. All of these arrived in masks to hide their true identities. They certainly provided first-class entertainment.

The condition of the track surface had become a major concern for the majority of riders. It was not being maintained to a safe standard. In a nutshell, it was becoming dangerous to race on. When a thunderstorm intervened on 14 June, racing was immediately abandoned. The track had become so dangerous that one bend was named 'Suicide Corner'. One young rider, calling himself 'MacDonald', caused a nasty incident on that corner by cutting in sharply on an opponent, who ended up on the grass. This resulted in a formal complaint, which was upheld and the race re-run.

Even admission charges of 1s (5p) and 6d (2½p), with half price for children, had little effect on tempting more spectators back. By the end of June, 6,000 had been the highest attendance, this was down by over a half when compared to the previous year. No longer were the star men appearing at Audenshaw. This was most certainly to the detriment of the speedway.

The first meeting in July began with fine weather, but a mid-meeting downpour left the track in a treacherous condition. Unexciting races were interrupted by frequent accidents. There was no respite the following week. A violent thunderstorm curtailed the meeting; the track was awash within minutes, leaving the promotion with little choice but to call a stop to the racing.

Track conditions were still a hazard. Not much seemed to have

1931 programme cover.

Audenshaw Speedway.

15th MEETING

FIRST EVENT 3-0 p.m.   GATES OPEN 1-30 p.m.

Official Programme 3d.

Officials:

STEWARDS OF MEETING	G. PEERS, P. BEESTON.
CLERK OF COURSE	J. T. WOLFENDEN.
COMPETITORS' STEWARD	G. PEERS.
MACHINE EXAMINER	P. BEESTON.
STARTER	J. T. WOLFENDEN.
TIMEKEEPER	T. LOCKWOOD.

Ambulance : British Red Cross Society (47th Detachment).

The Promoters reserve the right to refuse admission and to vary this Programme without notice.

MEETINGS EVERY SUNDAY at 3 p.m.

BETTING STRICTLY PROHIBITED.

THIS WEEK'S GAZETTE.

Upon reflection I think it would have been better for all concerned had last week's meeting been abandoned. Owing to the weather, two famous Stars that I had booked failed to put in an appearance, and their appearance would certainly have made a great difference to the racing on the day. However, Anzac has since written to me and he has definitely promised to appear to-day. He is undoubtedly one of the greatest Australian riders on a large track. Having in regard all the difficulties, I trust that you will pardon last week's effort. It is not often that I am guilty of staging such a meeting, and I can assure you that every effort will be made to vindicate the reputation that I enjoy for promoting real racing. Before leaving the above subject I wish to place on record my sincere appreciation of the gallant lads who did every thing possible to retrieve a somewhat hopeless position, and I will never forget Riskitt and Slider for their wonderful finish in the final.

Whilst the A.C.U. will not embrace our Track, they are always ready to embrace our ideas, inasmuch that they have adopted our system of handicapping to be used on all A.C.U. tracks. " Imitation is the sincerest form of flattery."

To-day, Mr. G. L. Arnold will attempt to beat Jack Wood's World's record of 64 secs. for the mile. He will use his Ulster Grand Prix Bugatti. This car is one of the fastest cars in the world. Well, Good Luck to Arnold ! Should this form of racing appeal to you, I will stage a match race next week between Mr. Arnold and another well-known Champion. I will be able to judge from your reception. I have spoken to the riders about the time wasted between races, and we can look forward to an improvement in that direction.

Several new riders are very anxious to perform on this track, and we can expect some exciting racing amongst the newcomers. Please be a little tolerant towards them. they must ride a lot faster than even Eric Langton if they wish to win any money. Incidentally that is the cause of the trouble between certain riders and myself. I am insisting that they ride for their money. There's no easy money at Audenshaw. Billy Brown and Dean are still on the sick list.

been done to improve the surface. Deep ruts could now be seen clearly. If a rider's wheel got into a rut, it was very difficult to retrieve the situation. The next meeting had perfect weather and, for the first time in weeks, no rain. 'Suicide Corner' continued to claim victims. MacDonald took a rather nasty fall there; he lost control and somersaulted through the air before landing on his back. Heavily bruised, MacDonald heeded medical advice and withdrew from the meeting. Billy Brown suffered similarly, but did manage to walk away from the scene. After numerous attempts, Frank Greenall's lap records were finally broken. How these could be broken in the prevailing conditions is difficult to imagine. The new times were claimed by a rider named as 'A. Douglas'. Allegedly, he was a well-known speedway star in the north. For the record, his new times were 32 seconds for a half mile and 1 minute 4 seconds for the mile.

For weeks, a serious accident had been imminent and it finally happened on 2 August during heat three of the Audenshaw Handicap. 'Jack Smith' (real name James Kenny) from Salford, was killed in horrific circumstances. Kenny had been given a 120-yard handicap. Having negotiated 'Suicide Corner', he was racing side by side with his closest rival, Edward Simon, an ex-Belle Vue rider. Not far behind was Jack Wood, who was a far more experienced rider. Jack had reduced his rival's lead to a few yards when, unfortunately, Kenny's engine suddenly cut out, causing the bike to slide sideways. Wood, who by now had closed the gap, tried his best to avoid trouble. Kenny was pitched into the air and landed on his head, but was trapped under both machines. Having picked himself up, Jack Wood rescued the injured man by carrying him onto the grass. The Red Cross attendants immediately transferred Kenny to a waiting car and proceeded to the first aid room.

James Wolfenden, the promoter, carried the rider from the car and, once inside the medical room, while lowering him, dropped Kenny onto the solid floor. He then rushed out and callously ordered the next race to go ahead. The rider already had a fractured skull and being dropped could not have helped his plight. Kenny was kept in the room for half an hour and nobody had the compassion to telephone for an ambulance. His brother, Tom, took him to the infirmary and remained there until the Monday, when James Kenny passed away.

The promotion was strongly condemned throughout the inquest. James Wolfenden, in particular, was severely criticised for his handling of the situation. He did little for his defence, when he personally called at the coroner's house prior to the inquest. He went to great lengths to explain that he was the sole promoter and that the track had nothing to do with Kenny's accident. The coroner, Stuart Rodger, made it clear to Wolfenden that he would expect an apology to be given in court, to apologise for this intrusion and he was then removed from the house.

On the day of the inquest, Wolfenden, although he was aware that his attendance was required, did not put in an appearance at first and entered part way through. A full apology was read out and accepted. Two riders who were in the fatal race gave evidence. Wood confirmed that he had tried his best to avoid a collision. He also stated that main contact had been with himself physically and not the machine. Frank Partington (MacDonald) also confirmed this evidence. He also agreed that it was Wood who moved Kenny onto the grass. When questioned over the medical room incident,

Partington declared that Wolfenden had dropped Kenny like a 'sack of spuds'. Wolfenden took exception to this statement and kept interrupting, saying that it was 'all a pack of lies'. For this outburst, he was fined £2, together with fees of £1 2s 6d (£1.12½).

When giving evidence George Cowley, an ex-Manchester rider, stated that the track was in poor condition. Cowley had been approached in the past by Wolfenden to race at Audenshaw, but declined.

Other evidence revealed that the safety fence could do very little to protect spectators or a fallen rider. On the day of the meeting, all appeared well until the clerk of the course made his inspection. On walking round the track, he could find nothing wrong. He then rode a motorcycle round the circuit and, to his horror, found deep ruts appearing. This was reported to Wolfenden but there was not enough time to repair the damage.

Even the attendants of the British Red Cross noticed the ruts and potholes. The coroner was aghast when the man who attended to the rider gave his account. While talking to Kenny in an attempt to keep him awake, he said, 'Bless your heart, no wonder you fell off.' The track was literally in waves, due to its awful condition. Further witnesses spoke of attempts to get Wolfenden to level out the surface. Tom Kenny had even volunteered to assist. All efforts were ignored, with fatal consequences. Another

The Snipe Estate, built over the Audenshaw Racecourse.

problem was the lack of marshals with red flags to stop races; not one was noticed on 2 August. It was noted in court that, up to that point in time, there had been ten fatalities in Britain and three of them had been at Audenshaw. The coroner, who had held the enquiries for the Rowlands and Owen incidents, felt that his previous recommendations had not been followed up.

The promotion considered having a doctor present as unnecessary, thinking the Red Cross would be sufficient to deal with any accidents. The inquest was dissatisfied with the treatment administered to Kenny by the Red Cross, who were censured. A verdict of accidental death was returned on James Kenny. Following the fatality, two further meetings were held. Although the crowds were up slightly, the racing did little to excite spectators. Perhaps the most exciting incident came during the last ever meeting at Audenshaw. A rider's machine burst into flames and it took another rider's quick thinking to extinguish the burning bike.

A meeting was planned for 23 August but the owner of the racecourse, Mr T.L. Owen, informed James Wolfenden that he did not wish him to hold any more race meetings there. This decision had been supported by the inquiry, which had recommended closure. Owen did not rule out a return of speedway. If it returned, there would have to be strict guidelines. As it turned out, the roar of speedway engines ceased forever at Audenshaw on 16 August 1931. The site was sold for redevelopment and the housing estate is now known as the Snipe estate.

4

DROYLSDEN

1927

Droylsden will always be synonymous with the argument as to where the first dirt-track meeting in Great Britain was held. The High Beech meeting on 19 February 1928 is widely acknowledged as the very first held. However, many in the Manchester area will take a lot of convincing that Droylsden did not run the first ever dirt-track meeting. It was, after all, held with the blessing of an ACU licence.

The land-owner, George Dodd, had moved to the farm on the Ashton Moss in 1920, with the intention of constructing a training track for his horses. At that time he was entering his horses in events at the nearby Audenshaw trotting track, which, coinci-

Droylsden trotting track, the site of the speedway.

dentally, was to stage dirt-track racing in the not too distant future. The first circuit built was a small one and he later constructed a second but much larger, wider track on the site of the original one. The second track was a full half mile, consisting of short straights and large bends measuring 230 yards each. Moorside Stadium, as this became known, was accessed from Benny Lane; locals called the area 'Worlds End', probably due to Benny Lane leading to nowhere.

The first Droylsden meeting, held on 25 June, was organised by Harrison Gill of the South Manchester Motor Club. Gill was later associated with Belle Vue in many capacities. Moorside Stadium was a rather narrow quarter-mile circuit. As for the track surface, that problem had a ready solution. Nearby was the East Manchester Corporation Power Station, which could supply all the cinders required for the surface. These were compacted into a hard surface, which did, unfortunately, affect the broad-siding of the bikes. Although an estimated 800 spectators attended, around 300 of these gained free admission. The riders acquitted themselves well, considering their limited experience of sliding a bike sideways and, as a result, some spectacular racing was witnessed, despite the inclement weather.

In all, there were seven events for various categories. Races involved anything from three to ten laps, making the longest race an almost unbelievable three and a half miles! One of the principal performers was Charlie 'Ginger' Pashley, who was the winner of the oddly named 'Experts Race'. He was later involved with Belle Vue as the machine examiner. Charlie was a respected and successful midget car racer. Fred Fearnley, who won the first race, was a well-known motorcycle dealer in Openshaw. He later appeared in the opening meeting at Audenshaw in 1928. Ron Cave the most successful rider of the day with two race wins.

All went quiet after this meeting and nothing more was planned or seen of dirt-track racing in the area. Even though racing really began to take a grip during 1928 in Manchester, nothing happened at Moorside until the spring of 1929.

1929

Advertisements announcing the re-opening of the New Moorside Speedway on 13 April were posted around the Manchester area. Admission prices ranged from 2s 4d (12p) for the stand side, 1s 2d (6p) for the popular side and 6d (2½p) for children. However, all was not well with officialdom. It appeared that the ACU was not prepared to grant a racing licence to Droylsden on the grounds that the speedway did not meet the necessary safety requirements. They were unhappy with the condition of the track, but even less happy with the non-existent safety fence. Acting on this, ACU officials posted their own notices, less than a day prior to the scheduled racing. Basically, it was to make the competitors and club officials aware that anyone, whether riding or officiating at this meeting, would be doing so against the ACU rules. Anyone contravening the rules would be banned from racing at any other officially licensed track in the future. The Northern Association of Dirt Track Owners had also received a telegram from Mr Loughborough, the ACU secretary, confirming this ruling. Immediately, they attempted to contact as many members as possible to warn them of the banning order. It was impossible to contact all the riders to explain the gravity of breaking the ban. The association decided to send a representative, Mr Albert Lees, to Moorside Speedway as a precaution, so he could explain the consequences to any riders unaware of the situation. Also present to oversee the proceedings were two ACU officials, Mr W.G. Gabriel and Mr E. Damadian. Both had travelled to Droylsden and issued the following statement on behalf of the ACU:

> The point is simply that it is not an authorised meeting, in any shape or form, and that any man who takes part, or officiates, is liable to lose his licence for open competition etc. under the ACU and be suspended or, if he has not got such a licence, he is liable to have it refused should he make an application. He would then be banned from any part in other meetings, TT, trials and other events under ACU rules. The ACU is the controlling body of all recognised trials etc. The ACU would certainly not license any track without a safety fence round it.
> (*Ashton Reporter*, April 1929.)

The result of these ACU notices appearing in the area did have a drastic effect on the attendance. Just over 400 people turned up. Before the meeting, all riders and officials gathered together and were asked, firstly, if anyone did not wish to participate. Five riders chose not to ride: Needham, Hartley, Cummings, Garwell and Ware. All others agreed to take the risk and go ahead with the meeting. Secondly, the organisers explained that due to the lower than anticipated crowd, the prize money would be halved. After considering this, the remaining riders agreed to continue.

Although racing went ahead, there was little incident. Mercifully, not one rider was injured and any falls were minor ones. Serious injury sustained at an unlicensed event would be the last thing the promotion wanted. The winner of the main event, the Droylsden Cup, was Tom Creegan on a Rudge machine. He was presented with the cup and a replica trophy by Mr T. Dodd from Chesterfield.

Later that day, Moorside officials made it known that, although the meeting had been scheduled weeks in advance, no warning was forthcoming from the ACU until Friday 12 April and, therefore, they could not cancel it at such short notice. It appeared that the promotion believed that the ACU required them to have three meetings before taking out a licence. They still fully intended to apply for their licence, with the promise of rectifying the track problems, as there was no intention of curtailing the operation so early.

Despite the trouble with the ACU, promoter, Frank Morton, pressed ahead with the pre-arranged meeting for 20 April. Aware of the damage caused by the actions of the ACU, Morton reduced admission prices to 1s (5p) and 6d ($2\frac{1}{2}$p) respectively, in the hope that this would encourage spectators to attend. How wrong he was! Obviously all the adverse publicity had disenchanted the public and, as a consequence, a mere 100 arrived. Thrills were at a premium, with the racing reflecting the mood around Moorside. Tom Creegan again proved to be the best rider on show, although, in fairness, he had very little opposition.

After witnessing such a low attendance, the landowner, George Dodd, announced the cessation of dirt-track racing at Droylsden. The only racing seen after that date was trotting races. During the winter of 1972, there was the possibility of a long track event being held at Droylsden, which was substantiated by the local press. However, it really did not get much further than the idea stage.

Opposite: *Moorside's final days taken during redevelopment.* Above: *A view taken from the starting area.*
Below: *Note the rich layer of dark cinders.*

5

SALFORD ALBION

1928

At a time when speedway tracks were springing up everywhere, it came as no surprise when an announcement was made, in July 1928, that a track would be opening in August in the Pendleton district of Salford. The stadium was situated on Cromwell Road, near to the junction with Lower Broughton Road. Prior to this, only greyhound racing had been held at the Albion stadium. On the opposite side of the road was the Manchester racecourse, the outer perimeter wall still stands today. A Stockport-based company, Albion Auto Racers Ltd, were the promoters. They also promoted racing at the Cleveland Park Stadium, Middlesbrough and later on in Berlin.

Construction of the quarter-mile speedway, which was within the confines of the existing dog track, did not take long. A composition of red shale and crushed cinders, to a depth of nine inches, formed an ultra-smooth track surface. Safety was of paramount importance and, with this in mind, a four-foot high sprung fence was erected. The lighting system used was of two million candle power and provided clear visibility for officials and spectators alike.

The opening night was set for 27 August, although it had been previously announced that racing would commence on the 18 August. As the track had not been tested, it was decided to delay the opening night. Amazingly, there were over one hundred novices who applied for trials. Torrential rain on the afternoon of 20 August caused the cancellation of these. However, by the evening, an efficient drainage system had restored the track to perfect condition. A sizeable crowd had gathered to witness this new spectacle and they were not disappointed. Experienced

A 1929 Salford programme cover.

racers gave demonstrations to the thrilled onlookers. Several promising novices emerged from this practice session but others, having tried, decided to call it a day.

The price of admission was 1s 2d (6p), 2s 4d (12p) and 3s 6d (17½p). A concession was made to the ladies, who gained free admittance for the opening meeting. Salford's opening meeting was a resounding success. Although there had been rain prior to the start, in excess of 20,000 attended. Everyone went home happy with all aspects of the meeting. Viewing the racing had been made much easier with the powerful lighting used and the announcement of results could be heard clearly in all parts of the stadium. In other words, the promotion had listened and learned from the mistakes made by other tracks. They had looked into most eventualities and ensured that their public witnessed a trouble free show.

The main attractions who had been booked to ride were Ron Johnson, the Langton brothers (Eric and Oliver), Stewie St George, Sig Schlam, Johnnie Broughton and Miss Fay Taylour, who was one of the few lady riders at that time. One rider, who obviously had a sense of humour, rode as 'P. Panther', presumably not in a pink riding suit! Eric Langton took the honours in the main events. He won the 'A' Grade Final and the City Hall Cup, which was presented to him by Clem 'Daredevil' Beckett.

Two of the riders who took to the track on the opening night had only been riding a few weeks. George Rowlands and James Kenny (who was a Salford lad) were later to lose their lives in separate track crashes at Audenshaw Speedway. The rewards available from racing drove these young men to seek fame and fortune. Remember, at this time, unemployment was rising and racing the speedways was a viable and exciting alternative for a young man.

At the conclusion of the night's events, Fay Taylour addressed the crowd. The spectators retorted with a loud, 'No', when asked if it was not ladylike to be a female dirt-track rider. Certainly, the public had taken Fay to their hearts. It may have been unusual to have a lady racer, but the race times recorded for her heat wins were, in most cases, faster than her male counterparts.

Such was the enthusiasm for riding, the applications continued to flood in from aspiring novices, all wanting to be a part of this new sport. This wave of euphoria also applied to the spectator. Season tickets were now being demanded and the Albion responded positively by announcing their availability. There was no shortage of takers.

The overall success of the venture encouraged an expansion of the racing programme. A Saturday evening meeting would now be held, besides the usual Monday one. This arrangement continued until quite late on in the season, when the Monday event was dropped. Crowds for the season averaged 15,000, far more than the promotion could have anticipated. Having this high level of support allowed Salford to book the top stars on a regular basis.

Fay Taylour, Ron Johnson, Eric and Oliver Langton and Frank Varey were all frequent and popular visitors. They knew the public had to be entertained and they made sure that they were. On a normal night, prize money averaging £100 was available; a princely sum in 1928. Another big plus was the condition of the track. Even though some nights were affected by rain, the surface remained in fine condition with not a bump in sight. The drainage system certainly was paying off. Riders could race with confidence,

knowing that they could pass opponents with minimal risk.

Ron Johnson was involved in one of the rare disputes to afflict Salford. Johnson had machine trouble and pushed the bike himself in order to take his place in the heat. It was during the race that Johnson allegedly cut across race leader, Flowers, and 'robbed' him of a victory. The other finalists declined to race against Johnson and asked for his disqualification. Faced with 'mutiny', Tommy Hatch replaced Johnson. Ron was having none of this and requested a meeting to put forward his case. He explained that it had not been his intention to cut across Flowers. The incident had occurred because of the speed he was travelling at. On hearing this, Johnson's opponents accepted his explanation. Johnson was a respected rider and his honesty with fellow riders won them over. Ron then proceeded to win the final with ease.

On 15 September, Fay Taylour, the 'darling' of the fans, should have raced against Eva Asquith, another prominent lady rider. Unfortunately, Taylour was forced to honour another engagement in London. Asquith did participate in several races but her progress was hampered by machine problems all night.

On the following Monday, Ron Johnson received a rather nasty injury. Chasing Eric Langton in the Semi Final of the Salford Handicap, Johnson lost control and was thrown headfirst into the fence and lay motionless. With the crowd fearing the worst, Johnson was taken to the first aid room. After a few minutes, he gradually came round but was obviously unable to continue racing. Ron also sustained a foot injury. However, a heartfelt round of applause was given when it was conveyed to the crowd that Johnson had not been seriously injured. The sprung wire fence had most certainly prevented a more serious injury by taking the impact.

In an attempt to get away from the individual style of racing, Salford experimented with an Inter Track meeting. A Barnsley team was invited to send six riders to compete against Salford. The meeting was run on a 3-2-1 points system over three heats. Salford proved far too strong and ran out winners by 12 points to 6.

Frank Varey also began to appear on a regular basis at the Albion. Varey could be described as a 'take no prisoners' rider. Rough, tough and uncompromising may well have been how Frank was perceived by his opponents but, by and large, his presence at a meeting could generate a bigger crowd. Some 15,000 saw Frank win the Salford Golden Helmet, 3,000 more than the previous meeting. Varey also took his fair share of knocks. In a mid-October meeting, he was racing flat out to catch race leader, Johnnie Broughton, but fell awkwardly. Frank got to his feet but then collapsed. Luckily, he was only badly shaken.

Salford's promotion was very appreciative of their public. One early October meeting hit a problem, when neither Larry Coffey nor Jimmy Stevens could ride. Realising that the loss of two star performers would be bad for business, they arranged for Fay Taylour to appear. She had travelled over from Ireland by ferry and after docking at Holyhead, she was whisked by a fast car to the track. Although she arrived a little late, the crowd were heartened by her arrival. They were treated to a series of match races between Fay and other stars.

An invite to race another Inter-Track meeting was extended to Middlesbrough. Again, the visitors could not match the Albion team, who won by 15-7. Harry Whitfield, a Middlesbrough rider, stunned everyone by winning the two main events of the evening, justifiably proving that an inexperienced rider could achieve success. Harry had only around two months' riding experience and had already raced at the White City Manchester Speedway in the afternoon. After making the short, four-mile trip to Salford, Harry went home with Golden Gauntlet and Salford Handicap wins, not to mention the £80 prize money. Considering Whitfield had never ridden at Salford previously, his riding was nothing short of remarkable.

The last meeting of the season took place on 10 November. Another Inter Track event with mighty rivals, White City Manchester, resulted in a defeat for Salford by 17-10. Furious track action thrilled both groups of supporters. On the individual front, Whitfield returned to win the Salford Handicap, together with the £40 prize. During the final race of the season, Harry fell when holding a good lead and was denied winning the Golden Helmet.

At the conclusion of a successful 1928 season, came the news that plans were afoot to formulate a northern-based English Dirt Track League. As two other local tracks, Belle Vue and White City Manchester, had already applied for membership, Salford registered their interest. Apart from Newcastle, Middlesbrough and Leicester, all the other participants existed within a forty-mile radius – an advantage when travelling to away meetings. When the official announcement regarding the formation of the league was made, Salford's application was confirmed. The intention was for the season to run from March to October. Officials and supporters looked forward to a new exciting era for the Albion.

1929

With the advent of the English Dirt Track League, Salford had high expectations for the 1929 season. Gone were many of the riders who had learned their trade at the Pendleton track. The promoters' fears were that no quality riders, like Ron Johnson, would be seen. Johnson had moved south and become an asset to Crystal Palace. It was hoped that he would be able to make several appearances at Salford, other commitments permitting. In fact, Johnson was destined not to appear at any Salford meeting in 1929. He received and accepted a booking late on in the season. Sadly for the fans, who still idolised him, Ron reneged on this agreement, leaving many disgruntled and disappointed people. His non-appearance was reported to the ACU.

The members who formed Salford's first league team are Sid Newiss, Cliff Watson, Tommy Mason, Cliff Whateley, Sam Higgins, Fred Williams, William Price, Henry Pearce, Billy Fletcher, Leo Kenny, James Kenny, Stan Wynne, Johnnie Broughton and Billy Howard. Average attendance in 1928 had been 15,000; worryingly the opening meeting only attracted 10,000. This trend continued, with crowds never reaching the dizzy heights of the previous year. However, those who did come along were treated to a marvellous display of broad-siding. The track was, as ever, in near perfect condition. A late cold snap had prevented pre-season preparations and riders' practice days.

Admission prices for 1929 were 1s (5p), 1s 6d (7½p) and 2s (10p), with ladies and children given half-price tickets. Compared to 1928, this represented a considerable reduction. Arthur Jervis, of White City, starred with wins in the Challenge Final, the City Hall Cup and the Golden Helmet. It was local rider, Cliff Watson, who gave one of the most spectacular displays of riding ever seen at the Albion.

Halifax accepted an invitation for a challenge match that was to be held under the rules of the new league. Salford managed a 22-0 win! The camaraderie that existed between riders was shown before the racing began. Local hero, Cliff Watson, had been injured at Belle Vue on the Saturday. News of his injury disappointed the crowd, until it was announced that Frank Varey had offered to take Watson's place. Frank, who was always welcome at Salford, received a generous acclaim.

During the course of the season, Salford rode a total of 27 league matches. Three of these, two against Belle Vue and the other against Burnley, were later expunged from the records as both tracks withdrew from league racing. White City and Warrington also withdrew at a later stage but all results against these two teams remained in the race records. Salford achieved 10 wins and 14 losses from a total of 24 matches.

The opening league fixture was at home, against local rivals White City Manchester. Salford could not match the awesome strength of the visitors. A shocked home crowd could only admire the demolition of their favourites, who slumped to 15-44 defeat. The teams on that day were Salford: Cliff Watson (captain), Johnnie Broughton, Cliff Whateley, Sid Newiss, Sam Higgins and Tom Mason. White City: Arthur Jervis (captain), Syd Jackson, Billy Dallison, Walter Hull, Les Wotton and 'Squib' Burton.

Salford continued to struggle during the first half of May. Another home defeat, this time against Warrington, was quickly followed by five consecutive away defeats at Burnley, Preston, Middlesbrough, Halifax and White City Manchester. Salford, now languishing at the foot of the league table, could not point to a lack of effort from the riders. They were meeting quality opposition and some of the away tracks were completely new to them.

Much to everyone's relief, the Albion gained their first league win on 20 May against Middlesbrough by 36-27, with a much better all-round display. Team captain Cliff Watson led by example and rode unbeaten by the opposition.

At this time, rumours began to circulate that Salford was to close down. Problems with the track's condition became apparent, but these had been rectified. John Hughes, the managing director of The Albion Auto Racers Limited, refuted these rumours and confirmed that the track would now be running meetings twice a week. Friday night meetings were going to be utilised during the summer period, together with the normal Monday meeting.

Leeds, who had already confirmed their league championship credentials, thrashed the team 46-16, but two days later Salford were equally dominant. Sheffield was unlucky to come up against the rampant home team. The 41-21 win certainly lifted the spirits of the riders and supporters.

Injuries, too, played their part. James Kenny sustained a broken leg, attempting to avoid a fallen rider. This was a major blow to the team. He had made rapid progress and given some solid performances in home meetings. To make matters worse, Cliff Whateley broke his shoulder. With these riders missing, Salford struggled to adequately replace them. Once again, the condition of the Albion track was causing concern. Some riders were decidedly unhappy with it. Urgent action was required to alleviate the problem. It was agreed that racing should continue to the planned schedule and track reconditioning be carried out on non-race days. The crowds were still holding up at an average of 10,000. Although the promotion was disappointed with the overall attendance, they realised that they could not afford to lose any more spectators, thus putting the viability of the speedway in danger. The existing bumpy surface was smoothed out with further deep layers of cinders being added. Once this work had been carried out, it returned the track to peak condition.

Everyone seemed happy and two further wins against Rochdale and Halifax vindicated the repairs. Preston broke the winning home sequence with a 32-31 win. Salford trailed by four points with one race to go. A valiant ride by the home pair narrowly failed to win the match. Nevertheless, both were 'chaired' from the track by their teammates and given a rapturous ovation by supporters.

However, the most eagerly awaited meetings of the season were against Belle Vue. Frank Varey, although he rode for Belle Vue, was probably the most appreciated visiting rider. Salford took a heavy defeat at Hyde Road on the Saturday and then managed to lose the home meeting by 34-29. Heavy rain had left the track in a treacherous state and it was Belle Vue who adapted quickly to the wet surface. The wrath of the crowd was felt when their new favourite, 'A.J.' Ward, who was relatively new to the sport, did not ride until late in the meeting. In previous weeks, Ward had been the star performer, winning many trophies and handicaps. The annoyed crowd could not understand why he had not been used earlier and made their feelings known. This Belle Vue meeting attracted an encouraging 12,000 attendance, the largest for some weeks.

In mid-July, a young local rider, Eric 'Boy' Worswick, made an amazing debut. Although he was only fifteen years old, young Eric still achieved two second places. Salford was never destined to be league champions – poor away form saw to that. At home they performed well. Leicester Stadium and Liverpool were the next teams to receive heavy defeats, by 43-18 and 41-21 respectively. Salford was now in a respectable mid-table position and some eighteen points behind the leaders, White City Manchester. The next visitors, Barnsley, were duly despatched back home with nothing. The 46-17 win was ultimately Salford's biggest winning margin of the season. Better still, Salford went to Barnsley's Lundwood track and won 31-24, resulting in what was the team's only away success.

The 12 August saw another lady take to the track. Beatrice 'Babs' Nield, a seventeen-year-old local lass from the Broughton area, made her racing debut at Salford against Eric Worswick. Babs, which was the name given to her by Salford owner, John Hughes, lost out to Worswick, but her pluckiness was appreciated by amazed onlookers. The crowd were not actually aware that they had been watching a girl rider until the race had finished.

Surprisingly, Nield had only been riding a motorcycle for eleven months. Babs, having two brothers whom had 'dabbled' with dirt-track racing, attended a Salford practice night with them. Her first laps at Salford ended in disaster, a battered and bruised Miss Nield somersaulted over the handlebars and ended up in a heap. To the surprise of many, Babs remounted the machine and reeled off a dozen laps without further mishap.

Nield was a member of the North Manchester Motor Club, who ran the Belle Vue Speedway. It then emerged that not only had she ridden in practices at Belle Vue, but she had also raced against Dot Cowley at Middlesbrough without success. Her father, a local coal merchant, purchased a brand new Douglas dirt-track model for her. It was not her intention to make money from racing. She treated riding the dirt tracks purely as a hobby. Leisure time was now spent adapting to the new bike and getting in practice laps. Later in her riding career, she was suspended for participating in races at the 'blacked' Audenshaw race track.

Tommy Mason, one of the mainstays of the Salford team, was to be married on 24 August. He wanted his team-mates to attend the wedding. So, to accommodate this, the promotion made a request for the scheduled league match at Liverpool to be postponed until a later date.

In the English Dirt Track League, there was also a cup competition and Salford drew Rochdale. The ties were to be raced on a home and away basis. Rochdale rode their home leg on 10 August and gained a healthy 16-point lead to take with them for the second leg and what a thrilling match it turned out to be. 'A.J.' Ward enhanced his growing reputation with fearless sweeps around the outside, which left the crowd gasping. His passing manoeuvre against 'Squib' Burton brought the house down. Despite his efforts, he alone could not prevent the 'Dale' amassing enough points to progress to round two *v.* Leicester Stadium.

Salford rounded off the home league programme by denting the title hopes of Leeds, who eventually became The English Dirt Track League Champions. The winning margin of 41-22 was a surprise result, as Leeds was expected to win comfortably but they came up against a determined home team. This confidence was carried through to the final home league match, with Newcastle being narrowly beaten 33-28.

Having made a slow start in the league programme, Salford gradually improved and finished strongly. Ten wins gave them twenty points and seventh place in an uncompleted season for the league. The Albion Auto Racers Limited made a shock announcement on 23 September that the track was to be closed early. The usual Friday night meeting was held on 20 September, but torrential rain swept into the area overnight and during the weekend. As a consequence, much damage was done to the track and it would not have been possible to rectify this in time for the Monday night meeting. It was on this basis that the decision was taken to curtail the season. They took the view that it was pointless spending money repairing something that would cease to be used in a month's time.

Salford's shocked riders decided that they did not want this to happen. A consortium of nine approached the promotion and Albion Greyhounds Limited with the suggestion that they would take on the running of the speedway for the duration of the season. The nine riders who breathed new life into Salford were Cliff Watson, 'A.J.' Ward, Billy Howard, Cliff Whateley, Fred Williams, Tommy Mason, Eric Worswick, Charlie Bentley and 'Cracker' Simpson.

Tommy Blakemore, an ex-rider, was the driving force behind this proposal. He was elected as a trustee, together with the fathers of Fred Williams and Eric Worswick. They would handle the financial matters and allow the riders to concentrate on what they did best. The consortium had to seek permission from the speedway authorities to organise meetings themselves. No problems were encountered with this and the approval was given at once. Immediately, the riders, with assistance from others, set about track repairs. Favourable weather helped them and the circuit was soon back to something like normal. The nine riders involved were not going into this blind. They realised that this had to work; in the past they had pulled together as team-mates and would stand together now. At first it was thought that one meeting per week would be held, which would be on a Monday. However, it was decided to continue with the Monday and Friday arrangement for the foreseeable future.

A 'Salford Night' was organised on 27 September to celebrate the reopening. This was to be a meeting for Salford riders only, with a special trophy being donated by two patrons of the speedway for the main event. The 'A and E' final was won by Cliff Watson, in a close race with Billy Howard. There was an encouraging and enthusiastic attendance, with the speedway's rescuers being warmly received. After all, this revival happened for the supporters who did not want to lose their speedway.

Disaster struck on the following Monday when the fates conspired against Salford. Atrocious weather again blighted the area and by the usual start time, the track was quite literally under water and the meeting had to be postponed. The new venture could not withstand many nights like this. To keep the track solvent, there had to be regular income.

Normality returned on the following Friday. Frank Varey readily agreed to help out Salford by appearing. Varey, as usual, gave a display of spectacular, daredevil riding but only managed to win the George Pemberton Trophy. In the remaining races, Frank failed to beat his race handicap, applied for being classed as a star rider. Varey had hoped that he would be able to ride at least once a week at Salford as it was a favoured track where he performed well. However, this was not possible. Frank had to undertake his commitment to travel to South America for a winter season of racing there. This came as a massive blow to the riders, who needed all the assistance they could muster. Varey did wish the riders well in the effort to keep Salford running.

More noticeable was the increasing absence of the star men, who appeared to be declining invitations to ride. Participating riders came mainly from the Salford area but this alone was not sufficient to hold the crowds at a sustainable level. Sid Newiss, who always pleased the crowd, was also absent as he travelled with Varey and others en route to South America.

Persistent rain over several days reduced the track to mud. Not really wanting to cancel another meeting, Salford pressed ahead. Racing was virtually non-existent, riders slid around, blinded by wet cinders and several crashes occurred. Tommy Mason and 'A.J.' Ward clashed due to the conditions; this allowed a local junior Peter Waterhouse through for an unexpected win. Sportingly, Peter refused to accept the trophy and asked for a race between himself and Mason to decide the winner. Although Mason

won easily, he felt, as Waterhouse had, that he could not accept the prize in the circumstances. A further race to determine the winner would be held during Monday's meeting. Mason was triumphant in the decider, Waterhouse led for most of the race, only to be passed on the final bend.

Meetings were planned with the previous promotion for the 1930 season. It was felt that Salford still had a future, if it was organised properly. Sadly, despite their best intentions, the riders' consortium had a series of misfortunes. Support began to dwindle alarmingly, a combination of foul weather and the lack of star attractions started to tell. Even an appearance in the penultimate meeting by Harry Whitfield, who was now riding for star-

Harry Whitfield, had a trememdous following at Salford.

studded Wembley, failed to swell the attendance. Low attendance had led to serious cash problems and a decision whether to continue needed to be made. Some of the 'nine' were very disappointed with the lack of support. By now Billy Howard had signed forms to ride at Preston, Cliff Whateley was undecided on his future and Cliff Watson had received a definite offer to ride at Wembley in 1930 for £20 per week.

Racing went ahead on 18 November. Cold, damp conditions prevailed throughout the meeting and, more importantly, the crowd was very sparse. At this time of the year, many riders had packed up until next season. So again, the event consisted mainly of local riders, which was partly the reason for a low crowd. For the record, the results of the three main events of the evening were as follows: The Corinthian Column: Harry Helsby; The Golden Gauntlet: 'A.J.' Ward; the George Pemberton Trophy: 'A.J.' Ward.

At the conclusion of the night's racing, an announcement was made that there would be no further meetings until the 1930 season, the main reason being the condition of the track. A combination of bad weather, lack of income and weeks of racing on an already badly worn surface finally forced the Salford riders to abandon hope of carrying on. Most supporters realised that it was only a matter of time before the axe fell.

Despite many meetings between the Albion Auto Racers Limited and the Riders' Consortium, with several ideas being put forward, speedway never returned to Salford. It was a sad end for a track that was so well organised and successful in the beginning but somehow lost its way.

Greyhound racing continued at the track and stock car racing took place there in the early seventies. The site was sold for redevelopment and a casino was built there. This was named the Albion casino, thus retaining a link with the site's past glories.

6
WHITE CITY MANCHESTER
1928

The White City Speedway was opened in June, 1928 and the season ended in December, with a total of fifty-one meetings taking place. Speedway in Manchester was only just beginning to take off; nearby Audenshaw had only lasted for a five-week period before taking a break and not reopening. The track was situated within the White City leisure complex, which was similar to Belle Vue. The stadium was two miles from the city centre with access from Chester Road, Old Trafford. Entrance to the complex was gained through two marble pillars, which formed an archway and are still retained to this day. Probably the only more impressive entrance would be the twin towers of Wembley Stadium. Close by were two other Manchester institutions, namely the Lancashire County Cricket ground and Manchester United FC. Obviously the challenge would be for the dirt track to compete against its more illustrious neighbours. At first, one meeting per week was planned; this was soon altered to two, with Saturday afternoon and Wednesday night events.

A quarter-mile cinder track was constructed within the time constraints for 16 June opening meeting. Race meetings were to be organised by the newly formed British Dirt Track Racing Association (BDTRA). Prior to the opening, expert racer 'Sprouts' Elder demonstrated the art of broad-siding to a fascinated crowd of onlookers at the greyhound meeting on the Wednesday.

The capacity of the stadium allowed 40,000 under cover, plus further uncovered accommodation, so the attendance disappointed all concerned, with only around 13,000 present. But these were early days and the expected upsurge in crowds was not far away. Charlie Dodson, the TT racer, officially performed the opening ceremony before the proceedings got underway.

It was no surprise that Elder dominated the afternoon's event, by becoming the first trophy winner in the Golden Helmet final. That apart, there was little else to enthuse about. In fairness, a majority of the riders were novices to the sport and had yet to find their feet. One particular newcomer was Arthur Franklyn who gave an encouraging performance and, very soon, was to become the star of White City.

The White City quickly realised that only the best would suffice to become a success. At the conclusion of the season most of the star performers had raced at the White City. It was quite easy to attract the crowd pleasers at this time. This was the only speedway in Manchester and there was no shortage of riders looking for bookings. 'Ginger' Lees and Tommy Hatch had raced at the earlier Audenshaw meetings. The experience of this allowed them to be competitive with the overseas contingent. Lees in particular rode stoutly and learned quickly.

1928 programme cover.

Tracks were always on the lookout for celebrities to attend their meetings. White City had an unusual and colourful visitor, Nana Sir Affori Atta, the Paramount Chief of the Gold Coast, who was introduced to the crowd. He needed little persuasion to leave the grandstand so that he could view racing from closer quarters. After chatting to several riders, he presented the Silver Armlet to the victor, Charlie Spinks. Spectators were by now becoming very enthusiastic about their racing; everyone had a personal favourite. Word of mouth recommendations spread quickly and crowds increased dramatically from this point.

New stars emerged weekly; the Drew family provided three of them. The best of the brothers was Albert Brendan Drew (Abel), who was born at Birr, in Ireland. He relieved Elder of the Golden Helmet at the second meeting and defended it twice, which was no mean feat for a rider of his limited experience. Even the ladies got in on the act. In a novelty race, Dot Cowley, aged seventeen, raced against her father, George 'Pa' Cowley. She defeated him and endeared herself to the record 25,000 crowd.

Star riders were now clamouring to appear at the Old Trafford track and many new trophies were introduced. Anything that the words 'Golden' and 'Silver' could precede seemed to be used. A system was devised to award points, according to the prestige of each event. At the end of the season, the overall winner of each trophy would be the rider accumulating the most points. Attendance levels steadily increased weekly, as new supporters were 'bitten by the bug'. Crowds of between 35,000 and 40,000 became commonplace.

Perhaps with one eye on the following season, White City began to arrange regular Inter Track Challenge matches. The first visitors were Barnsley, who lost 10-6. Sidecar racing was also popular with the fans, with extra races being put into the race programmes.

At one meeting, Fred Fearnley, a rider of considerable experience, had a rather unfortunate accident. After hitting the safety wire, he became entangled with a hosepipe and fell heavily. Undaunted, Fred took on, and defeated, the crowd's favourite, Franklyn, in the Senior Scratch race. Abel Drew continued his progress with yet another victory over 'Sprouts' Elder to retain the Golden Helmet. Incidentally, Elder had fallen, but remounted quickly and was reeling Drew in, only to fall again and eventually finish a creditable third.

The White City track.

Yet another 'hair-raising' character appeared on the scene, in the shape of Clement Henry Beckett, who hailed from Oldham. It was not long before the crowd gave Clem the nickname of 'Daredevil Beckett'. He was not a rider who did things in half measures; he rode on the limit and consequently received his fair share of injuries.

The White City track proved a difficult proposition for even the most experienced riders. Despite being a big quarter miler, the extra long straights gave way to very sharp bends. Quite often, riders would enter the bends too fast and find themselves careering towards the safety fence at speed. A clever rider would take the entrance to the turn much slower before accelerating. By doing this, riders could race closer to the inside line and still maintain speed and control. Franklyn was the master of this art and would allow his rivals to pull away, knowing full well that his opportunity to pass would arise.

After rather poor crowds at the opening meetings, dirt-track racing had captured everyone's imagination. On the early August Bank Holiday Monday afternoon meeting, a record crowd numbered 35,000. Just over the road, Lancashire and Yorkshire were playing a County Cricket match. Their attendance was considerably lower than the speedway. The noise generated by the bikes intrigued the cricket spectators so much that enquiries were made as to what was actually taking place. Later on in the month this crowd was exceeded once again as the dirt-track racing became even more popular.

The White City management now, for the first time, had a serious challenge to contend with. On the other side of the city, International Speedways had opened a track at Belle Vue. Initial fears that the track would affect them were quickly dispelled. The White City more than held its ground as it was now an established track, providing top class entertainment. Crowds actually increased during this period, despite adverse weather conditions. This encouraged the promotion to increase the number of weekly meetings to three, with a Monday evening being added.

When the crowd reached 38,000, many thought that a peak level had been achieved. How wrong could they have been! The Saturday afternoon meeting had always proved the most popular, but when 45,000 turned up on a Wednesday night, it caused more than a few problems with congestion on the roads and at the turnstiles! A group of riders from Scotland had travelled to Manchester to participate in a series of races billed as England *v.* Scotland. Harry Duncan, Drew McQueen and George MacKenzie lost the tie by 3-0, but endeared themselves to the faithful with some spirited riding. McQueen was unfortunate not to defeat Beckett in the Golden Armlet.

Clem Beckett was now a star attraction; to hold a meeting without him was unthinkable, but this very nearly happened. Clem had accepted a booking to ride at the Coventry track against Syd Jackson. Not wanting to disappoint the crowd, Beckett was flown to Coventry, where he defeated Jackson. He then took the return flight to Manchester to ride in the final event of the day. Such was his importance, racing was held up until he arrived. However, his luck finally ran out when a broken chain caused him to be flung from his machine, fortunately with no injury.

Another rival was anticipated at the end of August, when the football season commenced. Manchester United was at home on the same day as the White City meeting. For whatever reason, the crowd figures were not announced. Certainly, the attendance was nowhere near the usual level, but a conservative estimate was around the 20,000 mark. This compared favourably with the United attendance.

Handicapping was introduced in an attempt to give encouragement to the lesser riders. The calibre of riders like Franklyn, Beckett and Skinner gave the minnows little chance. By giving a handicap, the stars would have to earn their prize money the hard way, but it offered the others a glimmer of hope.

White City's management decided to promote a Grand Charity event in the aid of local charities. The proceeds from this were given to the *Manchester Evening News* and the *Manchester Evening Chronicle*, who funded charities through the White Heather Fund and the Cinderella Club. Other beneficiaries were the Manchester Royal Infirmary and the Red Cross Society. Such was the interest in this meeting, an astonishing crowd in excess of 50,000 swarmed through the turnstiles. A gathering of this magnitude had not been witnessed before at an evening sports event. Despite repeated attempts to prevent them, groups of people rushed the gates and gained illegal entry to the stadium. The police presence was powerless to resist the rush with around 1,500 breaking the gates to the popular enclosure. Luckily, once they were inside, their behaviour was impeccable and everyone enjoyed the racing. Arthur Jervis was a worthy winner of the Dirt Track Rudge machine prize, 'Skid' Skinner won the *Manchester Evening News* Cup and Jervis won the *Manchester Evening Chronicle* Cup.

Special guests for the evening were the mayors and mayoresses of Manchester and Salford, together with Lord and Lady Askwith. The crowd was thanked for making it an enjoyable event and also for the amount raised, which was eventually to reach £3,200 (a remarkable sum for the time).

Although three meetings per week were now taking place, it soon became apparent that one race day would have to be abandoned. It has to be remembered that, at this time, unemployment was beginning to rise. Several crowds in September fell below an acceptable level; there were between 5,000 and 10,000 on a Monday night. Reluctantly, the White City management agreed that the Monday night meeting would cease.

Supporters received another body blow when it was announced that the 'darling' of the crowd, Arthur Franklyn, would be racing away from White City during the remainder of the season. So dominant was Franklyn that he held most of the major trophies on offer. Talk of Arthur being unpopular became rife; the guilty parties were jealous people and the lesser riders, who appeared unappreciative of his skills. Franklyn was unhappy with the trend of riders ceasing to race when an opponent came to grief. Franklyn believed that 'a race was there to be won and, if your rival had fallen, then that was his concern, not yours.'

In Franklyn's absence, 'Skid' Skinner took over the mantle of chief attraction. However, he did suffer his fair share of defeats, something that Franklyn rarely did. Larry Coffey joined the White City ranks with regular appearances.

It came as no surprise that, when pressure from supporters finally paid off, Arthur Franklyn returned to White City in mid-October. A bumper attendance (proof that he was the 'King' of White City) poured through the turnstiles. He did not disappoint his followers when he successfully defended the *Manchester Evening News* and Golden Helmet Trophies. Even Beckett and the fast-improving 'Ginger' Lees could not halt him.

Star performer Paddy Dean.

The eagerly awaited match between White City and Salford was much closer than had been anticipated. Although the Old Trafford men won 15-12, the racing was of the highest order. Harry Whitfield, who was riding on a regular basis at the Albion, inflicted a rare defeat on Franklyn in front of an appreciative crowd. It must be said that had Skinner's form been as usual, the winning margin would have been greater. In the return challenge, White City led 10-5 before the heavens opened and the match was abandoned.

Rumours about a league being formed in the north for 1929 became the talk of the track, everyone wanting to know if White City would be represented. The fact that several other challenge events were to take place before the end of the season suggested that this was so. Leicester was the next to try their luck in Manchester, losing by 20-7. Coventry appeared, having already visited in September, losing 17-11. A team, billed as 'London', trudged north; they were effectively riders from West Ham and lost by 16-11. Salford came in a rematch and gave a good account of themselves, only to lose by 16-11.

It was decided that the 1928 season would end on 17 November as the weather had taken a turn for the worse, with some meetings coming close to postponement. This, together with smaller crowds even on a Saturday, hastened the decision to close for the winter.

A slightly bigger crowd, in excess of 20,000, attended what was thought to be the final meeting. Arthur Franklyn was crowned the Champion of White City and awarded the Golden Helmet to keep. Franklyn was given a rousing ovation from his enthusiastic followers. At the completion of the meeting, it was announced that there would be one further meeting. This would take place on 1 December as a 'Charity Broadside'. Franklyn won the *Manchester Evening News* Cup at this meeting, only to be dogged by machine problems for the remainder of the night. The beneficiaries of the proceeds were the Henshaws Institute for the Blind, the Stretford War Memorial Hospital and the Royal Residential Schools for the Deaf.

Over the winter period, news that White City was to race in the English Dirt Track League was welcomed by everyone concerned. Several matches would have been keenly fought local derbies but for the many problems that beset the league.

1929

The season began with great optimism, the spectators eagerly awaiting the prospect of team and individual racing. Arthur Franklyn had transferred across the city to the new Belle Vue track on Hyde Road, although the move dismayed a lot of his White City following. That aside, the Old Trafford outfit had an extremely powerful line-up and, over the season, proved a difficult team to defeat. However, circumstances were to cause problems at most tracks, with a few not lasting the course of the season. Despite all the troubles ahead, White City still managed to stage sixty meetings during the season. During the fragmented league season, White City rode a total of twenty-three league matches. Later, some of these were expunged from the official records as teams fell by the wayside for a variety of reasons.

With Franklyn riding at a rival track, it made the league clashes with Belle Vue all the more mouth watering. These two meetings had been scheduled for August, but sadly they were never to take place. White City opened its doors on 23 March with an individual meeting. Arthur Jervis won the principal event by winning the Golden Helmet in front of an encouraging crowd of 30,000. The management immediately began with two meetings per week on a Saturday afternoon and a Wednesday evening. Mistakes had happened during the 1928 season and they were determined not to repeat them. Perhaps the biggest error made in the previous year was trying to put on three meetings a week. During this period, attendance had dipped drastically on the new night and some losses were incurred. With this in mind, they decided to limit racing to two race days.

Burnley provided the opposition for the opening home league meeting on 20 April. They were seen as a real challenge and rightly so. Any team with the likes of Joe Abbott and Frank Charles had to be taken seriously. Thoughts of a classic encounter quickly evaporated, as Burnley was swept aside by 49-13. The away trip to Halifax resulted in a narrow one point victory, but a much better result came at Salford. In a surprisingly easy meeting, the home side capitulated and suffered a 44-15 thrashing, leaving White City sitting pretty at the top of the first league table.

Despite the one-sided nature of the early league fixtures, the crowds continued to increase. With the clamour for glamour events, White City issued a challenge to Belle Vue. The stake was £100 a side, with 'Franklyn's Mystery Men' being matched against the White City team. Salford were the next team to visit and, to be fair, gave the home team a good run for its money. In fact, Salford's 42-20 defeat was the best effort that any team would achieve at White City until the last league match held in 1929. The local derby attracted a record attendance with 55,000 packing the terraces. In the evening, the action moved to the Athletic Grounds, Rochdale. Here White City suffered a 36-27 defeat against a team they should have beaten with ease. However, normal service was resumed at Fullerton Park, Leeds with a good four point win against the team who were eventually to be handed the league championship.

Individually, it was Arthur Jervis who reigned supreme. At one stage, Jervis had five consecutive Golden Helmet wins, no mean feat against the quality riders who were

SATURDAY, April 13th at 2-30 p.m.
WHITE CITY SPEEDWAY

OFFICIAL PROGRAMME 6ᴰ

Next Meeting on Wednesday at 7-30

1929 programme cover.

invited to the meetings. To create a bit of interest, White City put up a £50 prize for any rider who could beat Jervis's track record.

Another major decision was taken towards the end of May when the Wednesday meeting was altered to a Tuesday night. It was a common-sense business decision, as Belle Vue also held regular Wednesday evening meetings. Neither track wanted to cause problems for the other.

On the league front, Hanley, Middlesbrough, Leicester Stadium, Preston and Newcastle tried to sneak the points away, but failed miserably. Perhaps the problem for the White City was the ease with which they won their home meetings. Even at this relatively early stage, it was difficult to see any team that was capable of preventing this mighty outfit from running away with the league. By mid June, the team had won ten and lost one.

A novelty relay race was held in June between two pairs of brothers. Arthur and Hubert Jervis were matched against Bill and Joe Dallison. The Dallisons held an early advantage, with Joe leading Arthur by thirty yards in the final leg. Arthur was having none of this and reeled in Dallison within two laps to record a comfortable win. Early in May, cracks in the league began to appear. Bolton had managed one match before resigning and was replaced by Hanley. By July, Burnley had ceased trading and rumours of a major rift between Belle Vue and the league organisers soon surfaced. The crowds had also taken a dip, with some meetings drawing less than 15,000.

Problems with the weather did not help matters. One July meeting was held up as great plumes of dust were raised on a dry surface. Not even a liberal dousing with water could lay the dust down. Barnsley and Sheffield travelled over the Pennines to try their luck; both put up poor performances. Leeds, their nearest challengers, failed to cause any problems, making White City firm favourites.

For a long time, it had been apparent that visiting teams were beaten before they arrived. In turn, this was beginning to reflect in the attendance. In the English Cup, White City was drawn against Warrington. Effectively, the tie was over in the usual fashion. The 50-13 win gave Warrington little hope, which proved to be correct, although Warrington did deservedly beat White City in the return leg. The reward was a second round tie against Newcastle.

When it was announced that Jervis and Franklyn were to meet in the £100 challenge races, interest reached fever pitch. Here were two of the top riders in Manchester going head to head. Belle Vue hosted the first leg, with Franklyn needing a third race to take a 2-1 lead to the White City. Jervis rose to the occasion and, by beating Franklyn in two straight legs, also won the prize money, much to the delight of the jubilant home crowd. Incidentally, this was Franklyn's first visit to his former home track in 1929.

The visit of Halifax was the last home league match to be held. Troubles were afoot which were shortly to throw the league into chaos. In July, Belle Vue resigned from the English Dirt Track League because of differences regarding payment and appearance money. Warrington quickly followed and rumours became common place that further developments were imminent. The NADTO, the league organisers, made it clear that any rider appearing at tracks that had withdrawn from league racing would be suspended from competing on other Association tracks. Many riders saw it as their

Jack Owen, 1929.

Scotty Cummings.

right to appear where they chose and several, including 'Dusty' Haigh, received suspensions. Although they were banned from league tracks, Belle Vue were more than willing to offer employment. In effect, the suspensions were rendered useless.

On 10 September, White City took the decision to withdraw from the league and the association along with Liverpool, although the Merseyside outfit later went back on the withdrawal and completed the remainder of their fixtures. White City should have raced against Newcastle on 14 September in the English Cup but, due to the situation, Newcastle was awarded the tie on a walk-over.

As White City had effectively won the league championship at this point, the decision was an unusual one indeed. Leeds, being the only realistic challenger, ultimately ended up winning the championship. The league strength had gone from fourteen teams in July to eleven by mid-September. To say it was a farcical situation would be an understatement and it certainly made it difficult for many organisers and supporters to take the league seriously.

For the remainder of the season, White City became affiliated to Belle Vue, allowing flexibility in the exchange of riders at both tracks. Talks regarding the formation of a three-division National League took place in Manchester, with fifteen Northern and Midlands tracks being represented, although this never came about.

Now that the two tracks were working closely, Belle Vue raced two challenge matches at White City. Although they did not have the cut and thrust of a proper league encounter, both events were well supported and enjoyed by the fans. The season eventually reached its conclusion with the visit of Coventry on 12 October.

A few days after the end of the season, Belle Vue announced the takeover of the White City track on a five-year lease. The previous owners, the British Dirt Track Racing Association, had suffered a series of misfortunes. These very nearly led to the company being wound up through the courts. The idea was to develop a new, even bigger circuit around the dog track, measuring one third of a mile. Remember that the majority of tracks working within greyhound stadiums were on the inside of the dog track. All the existing White City riders would remain with the new organisation, which was to run the speedway on behalf of Belle Vue. For their part, Belle Vue would only have the financial control of the venture. For both Belle Vue and White City, the main advantage would be the interchanging of riders between the tracks. This arrangement had proved to be successful towards the end of the 1929 season.

1930

During the winter months, a meeting was held in Manchester at the Midland Hotel, which proved very constructive. Its main agenda included plans to run the league on a sound financial footing. The northern promoters endorsed the way the Southern Association was run and unanimously agreed to the formation of a National Speedways Association.

Good news was received when Frank Charles decided to join the White City. Cliff Watson, who had previously ridden at the now defunct Salford track, also concluded that his future lay with the White City. They would be joined later on by Max Grosskreutz, Walter Hull, Arthur Jervis and Stewie St George, giving the team a powerful spearhead. For the first time, the team were to have club colours, the emblem chosen being a black diamond.

Les Wotton, who was a genuine crowd pleaser, had taken his riding skills elsewhere and decided to ply his trade with Liverpool, who were a lucky team to be signing a rider of his quality for the 1930 season. There had been rumours of two new venues opening in Manchester, but with money being in short supply in this part of Lancashire, it was not difficult to see why prospective promoters held back. During the weeks leading up to the beginning of the 1930 season, the teams who were to take part were announced. Many teams who had raced in the last campaign were hoping for better presentations. Mistakes had blighted 1929 and it was imperative that they did not occur again. The White City management discussed the possibility of holding Saturday night meetings and Belle Vue were happy to hold meetings on Saturday afternoons.

A new coloured lighting system had been installed, the idea being to replace the use of flags. Wilfred McClure, who was affectionately known as 'Fat Wilfy' during his riding days, was the man in charge of the 'New Speedway'. McClure was also the secretary of the North Manchester Motor Club, who controlled both Belle Vue and White City. The track had been widened considerably, and it was hoped that this would assist riders in achieving a faster and safer entry into the bends. The season opened with a variety of individual meetings, which were dominated by Charles and Jervis. Once again, the attendance was not inspiring, although this had happened in 1929 when crowds slowly recovered. An average of 15,000 did not impress McClure or anyone for that matter. However, the warning signs were there and action was needed.

In an attempt to boost morale and the crowd, former favourite Arthur Franklyn raced a series of match races with Jervis. The track was now different than Franklyn had been used to in his days at White City. How it showed! Franklyn was a pale shadow of the rider that used to thrill the crowd with daring inside dives. With the track now bigger and faster than ever, Jervis had little difficulty in seeing off his rival.

One criticism levelled at the track by many riders was that it was 'too fast'. At the opening league match against the Newcastle-Gosforth team, the visitors were demolished 28-8. The result gave credibility to the 'too fast' doubters. Simply, the Gosforth outfit were not equipped for such a super fast track. A three-a-side junior event was arranged between White City and Belle Vue. The event was not held under league rules. In the three-heat match races, White City won by two heats to one. Wombwell was swept aside on its home track, as White City won races with ease. Wins in this manner may have been good for the league position, but it did precious little to provide entertainment for the followers of speedway.

Much hype was given for the next home match; Belle Vue visited White City for the first and only time in the Northern League encounter. They won the match by a scoreline of 18-15; however, the margin of victory would have been greater had they not suffered from mechanical problems. Again the 11,000 crowd was a disappointment, although there was no shortage of excitement for those present.

The great Vic Huxley made a couple of appearances in May. Huxley had rarely ridden at the Old Trafford track and his presence certainly boosted the crowd. However, there were now rumblings of discontent amongst the riders. Frank Charles expressed a wish to move to the White City in Glasgow, who also rode in the Northern League. Figures approaching £1,000 were bandied about should the transfer happen.

WHITE CITY DIRT TRACK   MANCHESTER   1930's

Side-car racing in 1930.

Perhaps the biggest shock was the suspension of Arthur Jervis for his non-appearance for the league match at Glasgow. The missing rider did not prevent White City gaining a third away win, but did cause unease within the side. For the duration of his suspension, Jervis was racing in Hamburg. The ACU requested that the White City let them have details of the offence, which was done. The management did state that it was unlikely that Jervis would ever race for them again and could possibly remain in Germany for some time.

Spirits were raised when White City defeated Belle Vue 19-17, in the return match at Hyde Road. Although Frank Varey was unbeaten by an opponent, the overall strength and determination of White City saw them victorious. Frank Charles and Max Grosskreutz were also very impressive.

Not for the first time, complaints were heard. This time it was over the state of the track surface, which in fairness had never presented problems in the past. Riders were distinctly uneasy with the uneven surface and did not feel that they could perform of their best on it. The unrest was reflected in attendance figures, with many voicing the opinion that junior riders were not being given enough chances. This was a fair point but, in the cut and thrust of league racing, the promoter had to go with the strongest line-up. To do this, star men had to be included. To allow a lesser calibre of rider to face Belle Vue or Liverpool, for example, would be out of the question if the aim was to win the league championship.

Jervis, meanwhile, had settled his differences with the ACU and was cleared for a return to Britain. The White City management showed no interest in welcoming back into the fold a rider who had let the club down. Jervis would have to ride elsewhere to earn a living. The last ever home league meeting took place on 28 June, against Liverpool. A comfortable 21-15 win could not paper over the cracks that had appeared. A poor crowd of less than 10,000 witnessed the meeting and drastic measures were now being considered.

Belle Vue, who owned the White City Speedway, had never been known to tolerate losing money. The track was literally put on notice that if there was no upturn in the crowds, closure would be the only option.

Mindful of the opinions expressed over the lack of junior racing, White City and Belle Vue arranged for the youngsters to have a platform on which to show their skills. Billed as a 'junior Test match', both teams entertained all present. Unfortunately, fewer than 5,000 spectators passed through the turnstiles – this was a stark contrast to the halcyon days when crowds of 40,000 to 50,000 were commonplace. Despite protestations about juniors, it was obvious that people would only turn up to see star performers. Although it was not announced on the night, this was the last home meeting to be held in 1930.

White City, the team without a home, did manage to honour their away match with Warrington and scored an easy 25-11 victory. Walter Hull went through his heats unchallenged by any Warrington rider. Later on in August, they visited Preston and won by the closest possible margin; this time Frank Charles steered them home by clinging on to second place. This was the team's final appearance together and

White City, 1930. From left to right, Max Grosskreutz, Wilf McClure, Frank Charles, Walter Hull, Fred Strecker, Cyril Wilcock, E.O. Spence.

their overall record for the Northern League was 13 wins and 2 losses, from the 15 completed matches.

Even though the home programme had to be curtailed early, twenty meetings were ridden. In total, 131 race meetings took place in just over two years. Talk of the track rising from the ashes never passed beyond the talking stage. Many fans pointed accusing fingers in the direction of Belle Vue for not promoting higher-profile events at White City and keeping the top-quality riders at Hyde Road. The Old Trafford diehards would even suggest that the racing there was in many ways superior to any seen at Belle Vue. Although racing ended in 1930, a further meeting did take place in 1958. A Cavalcade Meeting was organised in June, consisting of speedway, stock cars and dog racing. This was the last time that speedway racing took place at White City, although stock car meetings were held in the 1970s. The stadium was demolished and a retail park built on the site. The twin tower entrance was preserved as a listed monument.